PRAISE FOR *WHAT IS REME*

"*What Is Remembered Lives* is a thorough, consid.
ating respectful relationships with goddesses, gods, ancestors, and unseen beings.
Phoenix's easily accessible approach will aid Witches of all paths, and at all experience levels, in safely and effectively deepening their divine connections. I will
highly recommend this work to my students and customers."

—Heron Michelle, author of
Patheos Pagan blog *Witch on Fire*

"It's not often that a book truly lives up to its title, but LeFae's *What Is Remembered Lives* does just that. This is THE text for anyone looking to strengthen
their relationships with the goddesses, gods, the fae, and the ancestors. Full of
powerful rituals, practical advice, fascinating histories, and solid Witchcraft, this
is a book readers will come back to time and time again. Highly and proudly
recommended."

—Jason Mankey, author of *Transformational
Witchcraft* and *The Witch's Athame*

"*What Is Remembered Lives* is a practical, accessible, and inspiring guide to rediscovering the spiritual forces intertwined with our human experience: deities,
ancestors, spirits, and other kinds of liminal beings. Through the mirror of her
own experiences, Phoenix provides a solid pattern that the reader can use as a
guide to build divine and otherworldly relationships going forward on their path.
This book is a welcomed tool for the Witch looking to explore the spirit world
more intuitively."

—Laura Tempest Zakroff, author of
Weave the Liminal and *Sigil Witchery*

"If you've been looking for a direct and to-the-point guide to working with Otherworldly presences, this is it—heartfelt, thorough, and packed with practices to
help you step into the living world of magick!"

—Sharon Knight, musician and
producer of Hexenfest

WHAT IS REMEMBERED LIVES

ABOUT THE AUTHOR

Phoenix LeFae is equal parts blue-eyed wanderer and passionate devotee to several deities. She is a restless seeker of knowledge, always yearning to learn more, dig deeper, and dive into mystery. Phoenix encourages the whims of her divine muse (or perhaps muses) to push her forward, which manifests in writing, ritual, teaching, and devotion. Her journey on the path of Witchcraft started in 1994 when her athame was a wooden-handled butter knife stolen from her mom's kitchen. Her love of magick and mystery lead her down many paths, lineages, and traditions. She is an initiate in the Reclaiming Tradition of Witchcraft, the Avalon Druid Order, and Gardnerian Wicca. She has had the pleasure of teaching and leading ritual across the United States, Canada, and Australia. She is a hoodoo practitioner, professional witch, published author, and the owner of the esoteric Goddess shop, Milk & Honey, in Sebastopol, California (www.Milk -and-Honey.com).

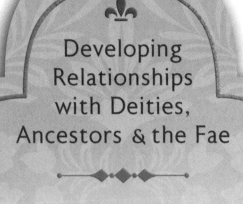

Developing
Relationships
with Deities,
Ancestors & the Fae

WHAT IS
REMEMBERED
LIVES

PHOENIX
LeFAE

Llewellyn Publications
Woodbury, Minnesota

FIRST EDITION
First Printing, 2019

Book design by Samantha Penn
Cover design by Shira Atakpu
Editing by Annie Burdick
Interior illustrations by Llewellyn Art Department

Llewellyn Publications is a registered trademark of Llewellyn Worldwide Ltd.

Library of Congress Cataloging-in-Publication Data (Pending)
ISBN: 978-0-7387-6111-4

Llewellyn Worldwide Ltd. does not participate in, endorse, or have any authority or responsibility concerning private business transactions between our authors and the public.
   All mail addressed to the author is forwarded but the publisher cannot, unless specifically instructed by the author, give out an address or phone number.
   Any internet references contained in this work are current at publication time, but the publisher cannot guarantee that a specific location will continue to be maintained. Please refer to the publisher's website for links to authors' websites and other sources.

Llewellyn Publications
A Division of Llewellyn Worldwide Ltd.
2143 Wooddale Drive
Woodbury, MN 55125-2989
www.llewellyn.com

Printed in the United States of America

OTHER BOOKS BY PHOENIX LEFAE

Hoodoo Shrines and Altars

Cash Box Conjure

FORTHCOMING BOOKS BY PHOENIX LEFAE

Walking in Beauty

To Gwion, thanks for always believing in and supporting me.
To Trinity, always go after your big crazy dreams.
To Bastet, the first Goddess I knew was real.
To Sojourner Truth, an ancestor of love,
a shining example of badassery.
To the Faerie Queen, for opening the way home.

CONTENTS

◆·◆·◆

SECTION ONE: DEVOTION

SECTION TWO: HONOR

SECTION THREE: CONNECTION

SECTION FOUR: PUTTING IT INTO PRACTICE

EXERCISES AND RITUALS

ACKNOWLEDGMENTS

I'm still rather in shock that this book has come to fruition. I have been teaching about working with deities for close to a decade. It is my greatest love. If it hadn't been for my partner, Gwion, urging me to put it all in writing, it never would have happened. To you, I am endlessly grateful.

I want to thank Ari Mankey, Thorn Mooney, and Stephanie Metz for helping me boost my (liquid) courage in even pitching this book. Thanks to Jason Mankey for seeing something in me.

Thanks so much to Heather Greene for being so easy to work with. Editor extraordinaire! Thanks to all the folks at Llewellyn that took the time to give their input, thoughts, and ideas. It takes a village.

I want to acknowledge and thank Gede Parma for writing the foreword. I am so grateful for your voice and vision. Thank you Suzanne Sterling for writing the beautiful Aradia song and letting me put it in this book. Thank you, Alicia Foster-Scales, for writing a powerful poem about Lilith and letting me use it in this book.

Thanks to the Godds, the ancestors, and the Fae. Truly, what is remembered lives.

FOREWORD
BY GEDE PARMA

I first met Phoenix in the Mendocino woodlands, among the mighty and otherworldly Redwoods, at California WitchCamp 2012. My first impression has remained: here is a priestess who knows something about spirits, about her connection to her beloveds in the Otherworlds, and about how to pull power and work magic. Phoenix and I are initiate kin within a particular tradition of the Craft and we are both public witches, spirit-workers, authors, and diviners. This book affirms and celebrates these things, as Phoenix's work and magic is further made accessible through the written word.

In the pages of this book you will find a clear and sound invitation into cultivating connection with the Spirits—be they Godds, the Dead and the Ancestors, or Land Spirits and Fae. And more than an invitation, here lies a model, a framework that you may explore and deepen into these mysterious and potentially intimate relationships.

It is clear that Phoenix is a thorough and focused spirit-worker, a devoted, caring, and fierce priestess with a desire to aid others in establishing and celebrating connections with the spirit-peoples. Her ecstasy and pragmatism shines through, and her retellings of some traditional folktales and grand mythological dramas provide new poetry and sensitively-attuned access. I know that I will go back to her words and read again of the trials and wonders of Vasilisa the Brave, of Aradia and her mother, Diana, and of the Avalonian Morgan Le Fay. I learnt new and intriguing things about deities I do not have relationships with, and this stirred my history-nerd fervour and desire to learn more about these beings that hold secrets of human legacy, culture, civilisation, and magic within their own mysterious origins.

I work closely and intimately with beings called deity, those who have died and become something different, and those land wights and Shining and Dark Ones we honour as Fae. Out there, in this world, I teach oracular and possessory arts to witches and spirit-workers in multiple continents; I help to bridge the void between animistic understanding and modern-day capitalist countries embedded within mechanistic and hyper-rationalist modes of thinking and doing. I was fortunate to be raised in a family that understands spirits to be quite real, magic to be an art and discipline, and the Godds to be mighty, primordial, and ever-shifting.

In reading Phoenix's words, I recalled how it was for me as a younger witch, taking steps onto the roads of these relationships and learning to navigate the Wyrd, refining my magical skills and my reaping the rewards of deep insight through the virtue of this good work. Phoenix's helpful directives and encouraging invitations support a deepening exploration of what I refer to as the web of becoming, that web of Wyrd that joins us all in the Becoming. Here is a book that supports and celebrates the skilled and radiant becoming of people drawn to the occult arts, to the powers of the priestess, and the haunting enchantments of witch-folk.

What is remembered lives: an affirmation, a blessing, a spell many witches I know speak aloud, whisper quietly, write on our mirrors and shrines…with love, gratitude, and deep communion, we light the lamps in our hearts with the oil of love, and with every heartbeat we further dance into the great spiral of life, death, and rebirth. This book, and Phoenix's priestessing in this world and Others, is a holy lamp, lit by the oil of love, that shines for those of us seeking warmth, inspiration, illumination, endarkenment, and the power and wonder of relationship.

—Gede Parma/Fio Aengus.

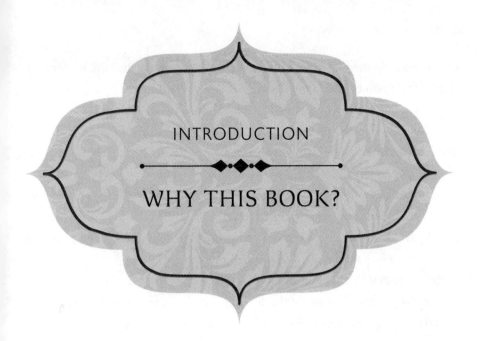

INTRODUCTION

WHY THIS BOOK?

In many Pagan traditions, we use the phrase "what is remembered lives." Often we say this at Samhain when we are calling out the names of our Beloved Dead. What is remembered lives is a way of honoring our ancestors, those we knew, those we never met, and even those whose names have been forgotten. By naming what is remembered lives, we speak to the real truth of immortality, because the only way that we can live on when we have left our bodies is if we are remembered.

This is a basic tenet of ancestor worship. We honor, remember, and take care of our ancestors so that they might take care of us when we are in need. We honor them, celebrate them, and tell their stories so that one day our descendants will do the same for us. This is a concept that can be seen all over the world.

In China, a deceased relative has a tablet created for them after the allotted time for mourning and burial, which can be up to seven months depending on social status. This spirit tablet is kept on an ancestral shrine in the home. Offerings of incense and food are made on a regular basis to these shrines. Fake bank notes, also known as Hell Money, are offered, especially on holidays and special occasions. The head of the household will spend time speaking to the shrine, keeping their ancestors informed of family events, and asking for help or guidance with troublesome situations. *What is remembered lives.*

In Mexico and many places in Central and South America, Dia de los Muertos is celebrated on November 1. During this time, families gather to honor their loved ones that have passed on. Often these celebrations take place at cemeteries following a parade that leads them to the site. Celebrants cook foods, leave offerings, and spend time at gravesites. Offerings for the de-parted are called *ofrendas* and they can range from favorite food and drink of the departed, to valuable personal items, to incense like copal, to elaborate shrines or simple marigolds. *What is remembered lives.*

In Madagascar, ancestor worship is still very much a living tradition and part of daily life. Elaborate tombs are built for the dead. These tombs are fre-quently opened and the bodies of the ancestors are rewrapped in silks. During the time of *famadihana*, or the turning of the dead, there are certain traditions of activity that must be honored in order to show the ancestors that you re-member them. Ancestors are given the first bite of every meal and the first pour of a new bottle of alcohol all throughout the year. Keeping the ancestors happy means that they will help you from the other side. *What is remembered lives.*

In ancient Norse tales, the power and talents of an ancestor can be passed on to a descendant, but that transfer doesn't happen automatically. In order to gain the power of an ancestor the descendant has to spend time on the burial mound of that ancestor to ask for help and guidance. Only if the ancestor deems them worthy will their skills be offered to their descendant. *What is remembered lives.*

What if I was to tell you that more than our ancestors need to be remem-bered?

Think about this for a moment. What happens to a Godd if no one is there to give them offerings? What happens to the Godds if their stories are no longer told? What happens to the Godds if they are forgotten? I know it is a little like, "*If a tree falls in the forest and no one is there to hear it, does it make a sound?*" but how do the Godds, Nature Spirits, Fae beings, and ancestors stay alive if we humans aren't there to remember them?

Many years ago I read Neil Gaiman's fictional book *American Gods*. In one chapter, the main character is transported to what was basically a god graveyard. In this place, he sees the shrines and symbols of hundreds, maybe thousands, of gods that have fallen to the ravages of time. Their worship had ceased, their priestesses were all gone, no one remembered their names, and so they died.

What happens to the Spirit of a Place when no one honors it, takes care of it, or shows it reverence? It's easy to think that a Nature Spirit goes along happily enough without human intervention. But there is more to Nature Spirits, Fae, and Spirits of Place than lone, remote swaths of preserved forests.

Have you ever been to an abandoned house? In my teens there was a beautiful old farm house on the outskirts of town. It had a wraparound porch, big bay windows, and chipped white paint. I was obsessed with this house because it felt so sad, alone, forgotten. When I finally made it out to that house to explore, I understood why it was so sad. What was once a beautiful thriving farm house was now a torn up, ruined, abandoned shell. It was painted with graffiti inside, unstable and damaged.

The house longed to be whole again. The house longed to have a family safe within its walls. The house was sad. I dreamed of buying it and fixing it up when I became an adult, not really understanding the true undertaking that would be. But the fire department burned it down as a test for their new cadets. Another life snuffed out. When I visit the land now, it feels haunted, forgotten, and unhappy.

How many Godds, Nature Spirits, and ancestors have been lost to time, invasion, and changes in culture? And more compelling, how many Godds, Nature Spirits, and ancestors are hanging on by a thread right now, only remembered in academia? How many deities are the footnotes of historical studies? How many Nature Spirits have been turned into folktales or fables?

This book is a call to action. *What Is Remembered Lives* is an invitation to find these spirits, connect with them, honor them, and share their stories. This means the Godds, the Nature Spirits, and the Beloved Dead, both known and unknown.

Before we dig into how to develop relationships with the unseen, let me explain what I mean when I say "unseen." Throughout this book I will use words like *unseen*, *Otherworld*, *entities*, and *the divine* interchangeably. When it comes to this type of spiritual work, there is not one true answer. With the unseen realms, one size does not fit all, and your mileage may vary.

I specifically use the term *Godd* to note a deity of any gender. It is grammatically correct to use the word *God* to describe all of the Gods, but the word *God* denotes male gender. The word *Goddess* denotes a deity of female gender. Besides the word *deity*, there isn't a gender-neutral word. Godd becomes the gender-neutral term.

I'm uncertain where this term originated, and I have tried to find a source. I first heard about this term from a Reclaiming Witch in the North Bay of California. I greatly appreciate this term and find that it feels better to use it as an acknowledgment of all of the Godds.

You will also notice that I capitalize words that are not traditionally capitalized. In this book, words like *Witch* and *Pagan* will be capitalized. This is done intentionally to give power to these terms. If we capitalize *Baptist*, *Muslim*, and *Catholic*, we should capitalize words like *Witch* and *Pagan*. I also capitalize the word *Fae*, which is done to show honor and reverence to the Fae beings I work with.

I am not sharing information from any one specific tradition. My background includes eclectic Wicca, Druidry, Reclaiming Witchcraft, Gardnerian Wicca, and Hoodoo. All of these traditional ways of working influence how I approach the Otherworld. The threads of these traditions are a part of what you will read in this book. This is my approach to the unseen, based on my training in these traditions and my firsthand experiences.

I am a polytheist; I believe that there are many Gods and Goddesses. I believe there are other entities that live in (and next to) our world, many of them existing just beyond the veil. Our worlds are like layers, connected to each other and with some influence on each other, but still distinct and separate places.

It's like a cosmic croissant. (Go with me here, I'm part French.) A croissant is a delicious, buttery, flaky pastry. When a croissant is made, the dough is rolled out, butter is placed on the dough, then the dough is folded and rolled again. Then more butter, then more folding, and so on. The finished product is layer upon layer of pastry. When baked, these layers sometimes stick together. Sometimes the layers form a bubble and there is no connection at all. But if you follow the bubble, eventually you will come to a place where those layers connect again. The layers sometimes touch and sometimes don't touch, but the whole of the layers is a tasty pastry.

This is like our world. Our world, the Underworld, the Otherworld, the realm of the Fae, even alternate realities all exist together in one scrumptious pastry full of distinct layers. These layers and realms connect and don't connect. There are places where they are closer together and places where they are further apart.

When I talk about the unseen, the Otherworld, the realm of the dead, or the Godds, I am referring to one of these layers. Some entities are excellent at moving between the realms and some are not. Humans seem to be the most challenged by moving from this realm, or world, to the next. But with practice we can learn to travel to these places more easily. We can learn to call out to the Godds, spirits, Fae beings, or dead and be heard. And more than just being heard, we can also enter into relationships.

It's also valuable to know that I'm a skeptic. I've had some amazing Otherworldly experiences and still had doubts. It can be hard to trust Otherworldly connections at first. How to do you know when a sign is a sign? How do you know when your communication with a deity is a true conversation and not something you just made up in your head?

This comes with experience, trust, and testing. I'll talk more about this in the following chapters. But remember this is part of a spiritual *practice*, not a spiritual *perfect*.

At the end of the day, it doesn't matter if you believe the Godds, ancestors, and Fae are individual entities, archetypes, or a voice from your own God-self. The messages that come through are powerful and valid. You have to be willing to put in the practice and test out the ways of working with the unseen to find the ones that are best for you.

Not everyone is good at math. Not everyone can run fast. But with study, you can get better at math. With practice, you can become a faster runner. Opening up to the unseen realms takes study and practice. If you aren't naturally skilled at connecting to those other planes of existence, you can become more skilled the more you work on it. From there, your encounters become stronger, simpler, and smoother.

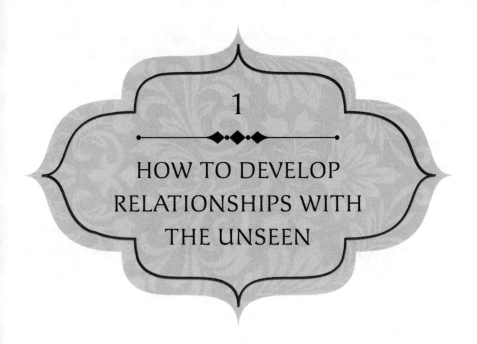

1

HOW TO DEVELOP RELATIONSHIPS WITH THE UNSEEN

When I teach on this topic, the first thing I address is the *how*. It can seem a daunting task to open up to mystery and to trust the experiences that come through. Folks new to this type of work are also worried about doing it "wrong," as if there's a road map that is clear, detailed, and easy to follow.

Being new to the practice of Witchcraft and Paganism, it is common to feel concerned about making mistakes. In fact, through the process of writing this book, I remembered being that new practitioner. I remembered freezing in that fear and choosing to do nothing rather than deal with the potential of doing it wrong. Too often these fears stop us from taking risks, trying something new, or stepping deeper into our power.

Let me make this clear: there isn't a wrong way to do this work. In fact, it takes trial and error to determine the best ways that work for you. To a certain extent you have to make mistakes in order to learn. Yes, some people are naturally gifted at connecting to the unseen realms, just like some people are natural psychics, but we can all become more proficient. It's not a matter of being in or out. It's more a matter of strengthening those spiritual muscles.

And, the paradox of that statement is that a little fear is good. We are talking about forces that are big, strong, and not completely comprehensible to human minds. Those entities that live in the unseen realms don't have the same levels of shame, morality, or boundaries that we might hold as human beings. However, that doesn't mean you shouldn't try, experiment, and take the leap. If something works for you, then it works. It doesn't matter if you've never been taught about it, read it in a book, or went through training for it. If it works, it works.

When it comes to working with the unseen worlds, you might discover that you get clear visions, like watching a movie. It might be really easy for you to "see" what others can't. You might hear messages, like a telephone call or a slight whisper that makes its way to you from the Otherworld. Communication may come through a deep knowing, a sense that you understand, but aren't really clear why or how. You may never see visions or hear messages, but you may get a clear feeling—an understanding. It could also look like a combination of all of these things, or potentially something else altogether.

There are two main ways of working with the unseen realms:

- **Realm Travel:** You travel to the Otherworld realms to gather information, talk to your guides or allies, and have an experience in—and of—that realm. Many folks would recognize realm travel as a type of Shamanic working or astral travel. It's a process or practice that magickal practitioners have been using for hundreds of thousands of years.

- **Invitation:** You call to the Otherworld with an invitation for specific entities to interact with our realm. This may include making space for these entities in your home, creating shrines, being in ritual, or sitting in devotion.

Although the Godds, the ancestors, and the Fae have their own realms and their own ways of working with us, opening up to communication with any of them is a similar process. As we move into the sections that specifically deal with the different realms, we will talk about the unique ways of connecting with each realm and the things that you need to be aware of. The following list is a good launching point for opening up to communication with any of the realms.

- **Create a Solid Intention:** Determine which of the realms you want to engage with and why. It's fine if you want to wander into another realm, but leave that for more advanced work once you are familiar. When you first open up to communication with the Otherworld, have a goal and a clear intention for what you wish to accomplish. If you are looking to connect with a specific deity, or entity, be clear about why you are reaching out for that connection.

- **Research:** Before you ever engage spiritually, research the entity. It doesn't matter if you are looking to connect with a Godd, an ancestor, or a Fae being. Learn their history, read their stories, and find out as much as you can about their origin and culture, including other practitioners' experiences of them.

- **Make Space:** Build an altar for the being that you want to connect with. An altar doesn't have to be a huge temple that takes up an entire room. Start with something simple and build as you go. This will give you a place to anchor what you learn about that spirit. Use items associated with the entity you want to work with. Choose colors, foods, trinkets, symbols, and other special items that will appeal to the entity you want to develop a relationship with.

- **Be Patient:** Time doesn't work the same way in the Otherworlds. Heck, time doesn't even work the way that we think it does in *this* realm. Developing a relationship takes time and it will need to unfold in the time that it takes. Don't try to rush things or feel the need to checkmark boxes of achievement. Just let things unfold as they need to.

- **Be Open:** The process will unfold as it will. There isn't one map to follow or one way to do this. Things might take off slowly and build over time or run roughshod over your slow methodical plan. Pay attention to small messages, coincidences, or synchronicities as you get started.

+ **Negotiate:** Not all spirits understand human consequences. As you start to develop relationships, set boundaries for what is and is not allowed. This is similar to any human relationship. "The Goddess made me do it" is **never** a valid excuse for bad behavior. You are always responsible.

A spirit may reach out to you without you attempting to make any contact with that spirit first. It can be powerful, scary, and even flattering to have a spirit reach out. However, just because a Godd or an unseen being wants to develop a relationship with you does not mean that you have to entertain that relationship. Always test the information given to you from a new entity encounter. Take nothing at face value.

What to do when an entity shows up wanting a relationship with you:

+ **Ask Them Why:** You are always allowed to challenge a spirit when it shows up. If a Godd taps your shoulder, you are not obliged to be available to them. If a spirit shows up in your life, it is perfectly reasonable to ask them why. One way to challenge any entity to see if they mean you harm is to ask them if they love you beyond all reason or if they are willing to support your work in the world. If they say yes, proceed with caution. If they say no, leave or banish them immediately.

+ **Set Agreements:** Set clear boundaries, and if the spirit is unwilling to work within them, tell them "no, thank you."

+ **Create Touchstones:** If you determine you want to work with this spirit, make agreements on how you will know each other going forward. A spirit, an ancestor, a Godd, or a Fae being may not always look the same to human eyes. Ask the spirit to show you a token that will confirm it is them when you encounter each other. A touchstone can also serve as a signal—or sign—that your ally can send to you when they want to communicate with you.

A note on being tapped by a Godd: Sometimes we Witches and Pagans make it sound like being tapped by a Godd makes us something special. This simply isn't true. A person may be tapped by deity for many reasons that have nothing to do with being a golden child. There may be past life issues, ancestral reasons, or something else that we can't comprehend. Pursuing a relationship with a deity is just as valid as finding yourself tapped by one.

So, how do we know that we aren't making all of this up? The short answer is this: you don't, at least not a first.

Many years ago I was learning a new tradition. My elder had very strict rules about what she called "scripting an experience." It was looked down upon to have a forced spiritual experience, to make things up, or to have what she dubbed as *non-authentic*. More than once I was shamed for having a "scripted experience." I knew my experiences weren't something I was inventing, but they didn't fit in the box of that tradition. I was so eager to do it "right" and have my elder authenticate my process that I never considered I was having authentic experiences, but they weren't the expectation of that tradition.

I can look back now and see what was happening to me was connected to my belonging in that tradition. My journeys and messages weren't "fake," but signs that I didn't belong in that practice. I was too green in that tradition, and too doubtful of my own experience, to push back or ask for explanation or help. I just thought I was doing it wrong.

Now I understand that you are your own spiritual authority. No one stands between you and the divine, and no one else gets to dictate your honest experience.

If your process is coming from outside of you, it is a valid experience. If your experiences are coming from your own subconscious or your own higher self, it is still a valid experience. You don't have to be a polytheist to work with the Godds. You may feel divinity as archetypes, entities, or something else altogether. Deity may be an expression of your own self. That's fine, your experiences are still valid.

What if nothing happens? This is possible. Sometimes nothing happens. This isn't a failure or a sign that you've done something wrong. Our questions won't always be answered. The Godds, Fae, and ancestors aren't always at our beck and call. Sometimes the phone rings and no one is there to answer it. This is true when reaching out to the other realms too. It's okay. Just try again.

Not all spirits care about humans or understand how to be safe and careful with us. More importantly, caring doesn't necessarily mean helpful. Godds, ancestors, and Fae beings exist in realms different from our own. The cues and signs that you might take for granted in other humans won't make sense to beings from Otherworlds. Communication may require more digging and discovery. Language may not be as clear or straightforward. Not everything is as it seems.

There are some spirits that may mean you harm. There are some spirits that are totally neutral and will not have any issues causing chaos in your life. However, the chances of a negative or dangerous spirit coming to you are very slim. That doesn't mean that you shouldn't proceed with caution. And there are ways to keep yourself safe. Here are some examples:

- **Test:** Always test any entity that shows up in your life. Just because a spirit says they are Grandma Beth doesn't mean they truly are. A spirit that loves you will not be bothered by having to pass your test. Some Godds may be impatient about it, but they will still do it.

- **Ward:** Set up wards and protections in your home and on your person. Wear a protective amulet or charm when you do realm travel. Have a shield you carry in the astral plane.

- **Allies:** You may already have spiritual allies that you work with. Ask these allies for their feelings about any new spirits. Ask your allies to come with you on realm travels. These allies will give you clear messages on who may or may not be safe for you to work with. Allies may be from other realms or they may be human.

The testing of a spirit can be done in your own Place of Power. A Place of Power is your own personal astral temple. In your Place of Power (or PoP) you can take objects you want to explore, seek out answers to your questions, test relationships with the unseen, learn more about the elements, the tree of life, and so much more. Your PoP is a place where you can explore endlessly and it will always provide more information, more details, and more guiding forces. A Place of Power journey can be found later in this chapter.

One of the important things about having a solid spiritual foundation is a willingness to be realistic and objective with your experiences. Any information received while working with the unseen realms must be tested and confirmed. Unless you've been working with an entity for a long time and have built a solid relationship, you need to test anything received. It is better to be safe than to be sorry. Never take action on a request given to you from any entity unless you know that spirit very well or you have tested the facts provided. The following are some ways information may come:

- **Dreams:** Messages may come in your dreams. It's a good idea to keep a journal or notebook near your bed. If you wake up with a dream fresh in your mind, write it down. If you wake up from a dream in the middle of the night, write it down. Even if you can't remember the imagery or the "story" of the dream, you may remember the feeling of the dream, colors, random pieces, and so on. Write all of these things down. The more you pay attention to your dreams, the easier it becomes to remember them and see the signs that come through.

- **Synchronicity:** A teacher of mine once said that if you get a message once, notice it. If you get a message twice, pay closer attention. If you get a message three times, it's time to take some action on it. Synchronicity is a concept that Carl Jung made popular. It is the experience of seeing patterns or messages in a series of seemingly unrelated events. Like thinking about an old lover and then turning on the radio and hearing "your song" playing. Pay attention when synchronicity happens; there are often messages in those moments.

- **Signs and Symbols:** Related to synchronicity is the experience of seeing signs and symbols. After working with an entity for a while, you may have a sign or symbol that you associate with that entity. When that symbol appears, it is likely a message from that spirit and worth putting some more time and attention into exploring.

+ **Trance or Meditative States:** Meditation and trance help to shift your awareness and open up your spirit. It can be easier for messages to come through when you are in a quiet, open, and aware state. Meditation is a practice, and not an easy one. Modern folks are often challenged to quiet their minds and sit in silence. However, much can be gained from quieting the mind and opening to messages.

+ **Altered States:** Trance is an altered state, but there are also other ways of achieving an altered state. Drumming, dancing, chanting, and even the use of drugs can bring about altered states. There is something to be said for entering into an altered state with the intention of making contact with an entity.

+ **Divination:** The use of tarot cards, runes, bones, pendulums, or other forms of divination can help provide messages and clarity on the work that you are doing with your guides from the other realms. If you are not adept with divination, get a reading from a professional.

Ways to test information received:

+ **Research:** The internet is a powerful tool. Look up and search for any bits of information shared with you from the unseen realms. Find any corroborating facts. However, if you don't find any corroboration, that doesn't mean what you were told is false. Keep looking.

+ **Ask Others:** If you work with other Witches, you can do some of this work together and share your experiences. When you have similar experiences you can trust what was seen.

+ **Astral Testing:** There are several ways to journey to the unseen realms. If you get information from a spirit, test it by going to your Place of

Power or using the portal exercise. (Both of these exercises are provided later in this chapter.)

A WORD OF WARNING: KNOW THYSELF

The first step with any spiritual pursuit is a process of self-exploration and self-awareness. Working with the unseen realms will challenge what you know about yourself, what you know about the rational world, and what you believe. If you take on this type of work without a solid base, a strong spiritual foundation, you run the risk of causing yourself spiritual, emotional, or even physical harm.

Things can come up when working with the unseen that can be triggering. The entities in the unseen realms work differently than humans, and although they may not mean you harm, they also may not be kind, subtle, or sensitive to your unique human needs. Be prepared to have your triggers flipped. If you don't know how to ground, calm yourself down, bring yourself fully back into your body, you'll want to work on these things before starting to work with the unseen realms. (There are some grounding practices in the Ritual Basics chapter.)

CULTURAL APPROPRIATION

It would be impossible to write this book without saying a word about cultural appropriation. There are deities that have an unbroken lineage of worship. There are deities that have been worshipped by living traditions for hundreds and thousands of years. For the most part, these traditions are cultural, meaning you can't just jump in and become a practitioner. In some parts of the world where Hinduism is practiced, you can't convert to Hinduism. You either are a Hindu or you're not. There are many African and Afro-Caribbean traditions that are cultural, but you can convert into them if you've been properly initiated. There are Asian deities that are woven into the daily culture of a certain region, and without living in this region your connection to this deity would be considered by many to be inappropriate.

You may be called to Godds that are not of your ancestral lineage. You may be called to deities that are from different countries. This is not wrong. But if you find yourself called to a Godd from a living tradition, approach this deity with respect, not only for the Godd, but for the people and the culture they come from.

This means that you may have to find a way to travel to that part of the world. You may have to go through a long initiation process. You may have to get permission from spiritual leaders in that lineage to work with that Godd. It may take longer and there may be more expectations on you. This can feel hard; especially for white Westerners who are used to having access to anything and everything. But trust me: approaching a living tradition with reverence and proper respect is worth it. It will give you a genuine experience and access to leaders in a living tradition that can guide you through the twists and turns of working with their Godds.

PLACE OF POWER

Once you open the door to your Place of Power, it can be used as a jumping off point for all other spiritual work. In this book, there are a series of journeys that start from your PoP. It will provide you with endless trails to follow. The secret homes, grottoes, and dwelling places of the Godds, ancestors, and Fae that you want to commune with will be accessible in your PoP. This place will continue to unfold as you need it to. Each time you seek out a new location, the path will reveal itself and will remain available as long as you desire it.

The best way to work through the journeys in this book is to have a friend or coven mate lead you through the journey, but you don't have to work with others to have a successful experience. You can easily record yourself reading the trance journeys and listen to them later. Read the trances slowly, leaving space between the words. Pause as you move through the journey, allowing things to unfold while you are in the other realms.

When going on a trance journey, find a time and place where you will be undisturbed. Make yourself comfortable. You may want to lie down, but I encourage you to sit up with your feet flat on the floor. During the journey, keep a journal and pen close by. Afterward, write down anything important, interesting, or curious that may have happened. Also have a glass of water handy and drink it upon your return.

When going into trance, you need an induction to help you shift from this realm into other realms. There are lots of ways to shift your awareness, and I encourage you to test out lots of inductions. I've included in this chapter a basic induction that can be used for all of the trance journeys that will follow.

TRANCE INTRO

Give yourself the luxury of a breath. Breathe in and out as you normally do, noticing the ease of the flow. Notice the natural pause between your inhalation and exhalation. Just notice, allowing your breath to come as it wants. As you follow this breath, shift your awareness to your toes. Surround your toes with a bright warm light. This light releases your muscles and relaxes your cells.

This warmth, this bright light travels up your body. The light swirls around your ankles, releasing and relaxing as it moves up your body. This light travels up around your shins and your calves, warming your muscles, leaving your body relaxed. This light surrounds your knees and flows upward, warming your thighs, releasing and relaxing, warming up every cell, tendon, and muscle.

The light continues to flow upward, swirling around your hips and buttocks, filling up your pelvic bowl. This bright light continues to move up your body, warming your belly and your lower back. The warmth, the light, flows up your spine, your sacred flute. The warmth releases and relaxes all of the cells in your body.

Up your body the warm light continues to swirl and caress. It flows up your rib cage, warming your heart and flowing across your chest. The warmth swirls around your arms, your shoulders, releasing and relaxing, filling every cell. This light swirls down your arms, warming your triceps and biceps. The light swirls around your elbows and moves down your forearms. The warmth, the light, flows into your hands, releasing your muscles and relaxing your body. The light flows into and out of every single fingertip.

The warmth, the light, continues to flow up your neck, along your jawline, and fills up your skull. The bright light touches your cheeks, swirls around your ears, flows over your nose, eyes, and temples. This bright light swirls around, closing itself at the top of your head. Leaving your whole body warm, relaxed, and released.

From this place of pure relaxation, open your inner eye, your Witch's eye that sits just above and between your normal seeing eyes…

Now you are ready to move into a trance journey.

PLACE OF POWER TRANCE

Before you is a door. With your inner eye, allow this door to become firm, clear, and solid in form and shape. What is this door made of? How large or small is it? What is its color? Are there any distinguishing markings or designs on it? What does the door handle look like? Allow this magickal door to come fully into life, allow the door to become firm and solid. This is the door that will take you to your Place of Power. You will return to this place many times and for many reasons.

When the door is clear and solid, knock three times and open the door, stepping into your Place of Power.

Now you step out of the doorway into the center of your land. All around you is your own magickal landscape. This is the realm of you. Travel to the east of this land and see what awaits you. What does the east look like in your Place of Power? Explore this part of your land. (Pause...)

Travel to the south of your Place of Power and see what awaits you here. What does the south look like in your land? Take some time to explore the south. (Pause...)

Move to the west in your land. What does the west look like in your Place of Power? Explore this part of your personal landscape. (Pause...)

Travel now to the north in your Place of Power. What does it look like here? Explore the north in your land. (Pause...)

Move to the center of your land. What is here in the middle of it all? Perhaps you want to create something here—a sanctuary, a room, a tree—where you can come and rest and reflect on what you experience. (Pause...) Also in this space is your doorway. The door that brought you into this land and the door that will take you back to your body.

When you feel ready, knowing that you can return to your Place of Power at any time, step back through the doorway. Close the door and close your inner eye.

Take a moment to reconnect with your body. Notice your breathing. Take a moment to notice your feet, your hips, your shoulders, and the top of your head. Slowly open your eyes and take in the space around you. Tap the edges of your body and say your name out loud three times.

Once you have returned fully to your body, drink the glass of water and take time to write down your experience. Include any important markers or images that came through in your Place of Power. Perhaps draw a map to help you remember the layout of your land and engage your child self.

2

RITUAL BASICS

The rituals in this book are based in modern Wicca and Witchcraft practices. If you are familiar with modern Wiccan ritual, the words and form of these rituals will be familiar to you. If these forms of rituals are new to you, this chapter will fill in all you need to know to create these rituals with ease.

All the rituals will follow this format:

1. Set Up

2. Grounding/Cleansing

3. Creating Sacred Space

4. The "Working"

5. Releasing Sacred Space

If your tradition uses specific processes, language, or forms to create sacred space, you are welcome to change up the format here for your own use. Each ritual is slightly different and unique. The creation process and ritual format are all slightly varied. This chapter will be laid out following the bullet points above.

SET UP

Every ritual will start with a list of items you will need to complete the ritual. In some cases, an anointing oil or incense is suggested. Please make sure that you test for any allergy before using the suggested herbs or formulas. Where alcohol is suggested, you can trade that out for juice if you so choose. Always make adjustments to the ritual items for your own health and safety.

GROUNDING PRACTICE

Grounding and centering is a practice of consciously fully inhabiting your body. You might think that we are always fully inhabiting our bodies, but we rarely are. We get distracted, our thoughts may wander, we may find that we are thinking about grocery shopping when we are attempting to step into the mystery of a ritual. Grounding and centering can help us to get into the right space—mentally and physically—for ritual.

If you already have a strong grounding or centering practice, perfect! Use that! If not, here are some techniques to try out and fold into your practice.

In cultures all over the world you can find the concept of physical energy centers. Different regions put these energy centers in different places, but there are more similarities than differences. Understanding how your body and your energy centers work will help you ground and recalibrate more easily.

In other parts of the world there is a repeating pattern of three main energy centers in the body. The three energy centers overlay quite perfectly with the Jungian concept of the triple soul. The first body of the triple soul in Jungian psychology is the Id. The Id is our primal self. It is our connection to the animal body that we live in. The Id is also referred to as our child self. It needs to be taken care of like a child, but it is also primal, a bit wild, and feral. This part of our self has direct connection to our God-self.

The second part of our triple soul is the Ego, sometimes called the talking self. The Ego is the typical voice in our head. It is there to protect us. It has learned from our life experiences and seeks to keep us from being hurt. However, in its desire to protect it can sometimes keep us stuck in old patterns. The Ego keeps our primal self and God-self from talking to each other. It has to be kept occupied in order for those other two selves to get anything remotely spiritual done.

Lastly, you have the Super-ego or the unconsciousness, also called the God-self. This is the piece of us that is connected to the collective unconscious. It is through this self that we are able to connect to the divine realms. This is where our God-selves live and can communicate with the divine beings greater than our humanness.

TRIPLE SOUL ALIGNMENT

The triple soul alignment comes from the Anderson Feri Tradition, and in the Reclaiming Tradition we use an adaptation of it. It has been written about many times by teachers in the Feri Tradition, and each practitioner has a slightly different way of going through the process. Here is how I use the triple soul alignment:

THE EXERCISE

Stand with your feet apart. Feel your feet rooted to the ground. Allow that rooted feeling to help you sink into your connection with the earth. Breathe in deeply and allow that breath to fill up your belly. Continue to breathe deeply, filling your belly until it feels alive with the energy of your breath.

When ready, shift your focus and breathe in deep, filling up your heart. Continue to breathe into your heart space, awakening those cells and molecules with your breath. When you feel full of energy, when you feel full of your own breath, take in one final deep breath. On your exhale, tilt your head up and offer that breath to your God-self.

This breath can be done upon rising, before going to bed, after an intense ritual, or any time you need extra help centering or coming more fully into your body.

CAULDRONS ALIGNMENT

"The Cauldron of Posey" is an ancient Irish poem. In the writings there is a description of three internal cauldrons that are a part of every human body. Much like the triple soul, these energy centers bring different facets of ourselves together and provide us with different pieces information. These energy centers can be worked with to help you better integrate your power.

The first cauldron is called the Cauldron of Warming and it sits in your pelvic bowl. This is the energy center that connects you to all your base/basic human needs. This is where your energy for home, comfort, and care resides. What this cauldron looks like, the color of the brew, and the amount of brew available should all be taken into consideration.

The second of the cauldrons is the Cauldron of Vocation and it sits in your heart. This cauldron is typically tipped over on its side, allowing for the contents to flow out and over. There is where your energy around love, relationships, communication, and connection all resides. What this cauldron looks like, the color of the brew, and the amount of brew being sustained in this cauldron should also be looked at.

Finally there is the Cauldron of Wisdom. This cauldron is the top of your skull. It is tipped over, and occasionally when we connect to divinity this cauldron will right itself and fill with a brew. This is not sustaining, but we get deep downloads and spiritual information when it does turn upright. What this cauldron is made out of, the brew, and how much brew fills the cauldron should all be looked at for information.

THE EXERCISE

Stand up and breathe in deeply. Draw energy up from the earth and allow it to flow into your body. Continue to breathe, pulling the energy higher and higher until you reach your pelvic bowl. Allow the earth energy to awaken and aliven this energy center, the Cauldron of Warming. Take note of the shape, color, and material of the cauldron that lives in your pelvic bowl. Take note of the color and viscosity of the brew. If your brew needs filling, breathe into it, pulling up earth energy, and fill that cauldron.

Let this breathing continue, drawing your breath up to the Cauldron of Vocation in your heart. Share your breath with this cauldron. Take note of the shape, color, and material this cauldron is made of. Take note of the brew and if it needs filling. Breathe into the cauldron, allowing any cracks or weakness to be strengthened. Share your breath with the brew, allowing it to fill.

Continue to pull the breath upward to the cauldron at the top of your head. The Cauldron of Wisdom. This is the cauldron that shares space with your skull. Breathe into this cauldron and see if you can turn it right side up, even if only for a moment. Take note of the material, size, and color of this cauldron. Take note of the brew and breathe into this cauldron, filling it up.

Hold this for a moment, allowing all of your cauldrons to be in alignment. Feel their power. Let their power expand and fill your body and your aura beyond the physical. Open your eyes and feel this energy holding you up and keeping you strong.

CHAKRA ALIGNMENT

The chakra system comes from India, but the influence of this system has spread across the globe. Many folks, even people who don't have a spiritual practice, have heard the word *chakra*. In this system there are seven main energy centers, starting between the legs and ending at the top of the head. However, in this system there are also hundreds of other chakra energy centers throughout the body. The more you work with chakras, the more you will be able to feel and connect with some of the more subtle energies in your body. When doing intense spiritual work, checking in with your main chakras can help you to ground and reconnect to your body.

If you've not done any work with the chakras in the past, try the following exercise slowly. You might consider having someone lead you through this process a few times until it is comfortable for you to do on your own. As you get used to the movement of energy you can do it more quickly. As you become proficient with this working you can do this process in a minute.

THE EXERCISE

This can be done slowly, taking time with each energy center, or it can be done quickly, like a scan of your body. Stand or sit with your spine straight and close your eyes. Breathe in deeply and remember your connection to the earth below you. When you feel ready, breathe in, drawing up the earth energy into your first chakra, your root chakra, right between your legs. This first energy center is red in color. It is like a glowing orb of red that sits right at the base of your body. This center is connected to security and basic human needs. Let this red orb fill with earth energy.

When you feel ready, breathe in, drawing that energy up along your body into your pelvic bowl. This is the place where your sacral chakra sits. This energy center is an orange orb, connected to sexuality and relationships. Breathe in and allow the earth energy to fill up this orb, helping it to glow more brightly and clear away anything stuck.

As you breathe, draw that earth energy up again into your solar plexus. This is the seat of a glowing yellow orb. This energy center is the seat of your willpower. Breathe in and allow the earth energy to flow upward, filling this yellow orb. Allow this place to glow and clear.

Breathe upward, pulling that earth power into your heart. This is the seat of your heart chakra, which is a green orb. This is the seat of your love and connection to others. Allow your breath and the earth energy to fill this space, clearing as your breath fills you.

When you are ready again, pull the energy upward into your throat. This orb is a brilliant blue. This is the place of your throat chakra, which is connected to communication and speaking your truth. Breathe in, allowing the energy of the earth to flow upward, filling this place.

Again, allow your breath to pull the earth energy up into your third eye, that spot just above and between your regular seeing eyes. This energy center is a deep purple. This is the seat of your intuition and clear knowing. Let your breath clear out this space.

Finally, draw that energy up to the top of your head. This is the seat of your crown chakra. This is the place of connection to divinity. The energy center here is ultra-violet, so purple it is almost white. Breathe the earth energy up to this space and allow your breathing to clear out the energy center, filling it up.

Allow yourself to be a clear channel for just a moment. Let the energy of the earth flow through you, connecting to each of your chakra centers. Breathe deeply, feeling yourself full and grounded. As you feel ready, dampen the connection to the earth, allow your breathing to return to normal, and open your eyes.

AURA WIPE DOWN

We have our physical body and then we have several layers of etheric bodies that live in and around our physical body. Sometimes things can get stuck in our auras. Just walking around in the world can make us spiritually dirty. It's just part of being human. Actively clearing the aura on a regular basis is just good spiritual hygiene.

There are several ways to clear your aura or do a quick cleanse, which ultimately helps you ground and center yourself.

The following list is a jumping off point. I encourage you to expand on this list. Find the things that work for you. A spiritual practice is just that: a practice. Try things out and experiment to discover what works best for you and your body.

- **Smudge:** Burning herbs like sage, cedar, or Palo Santo is a great way to cleanse your non-physical body. But don't think that you have to stick with sage. Smudging can be done with a wide variety of herbs and resins. With a little research, you may discover an herb that is in alignment with your spiritual working, your zodiac sign, or the energy you are working to manifest more fully. Try out other herbs and see what works best for you.

- **Shake:** Shaking your body is a powerful way to cleanse and shift your awareness back into your body. I like to compare this to being an opossum. When opossums are attacked they play dead, but once the danger has passed, they physically re-enact the scenario, moving through the "trauma" of the experience. Shaking your body like a dog that just got out of the bath can allow you to center yourself and clear things out of your etheric bodies that you don't need.

- **Rattle or Drum:** Using a rattle or drum on your body can help clear your aura and allow you to ground at the same time. My favorite cleanse is one that I call the "double drum cleanse." You need three people. One stands in the center, while the two others stand to the front and back of the first person, holding a frame drum toward the person in the center. The drummers do a rapid drum rhythm, following each other up and down the center person's body. It is quick and powerful.

◆ **Aura Comb:** If you need a good aura cleanse and you're with a group of people, start an aura combing. Have one person stand in the center of the group while each other person helps to clear and comb out their aura. The "combers" use their hands to seek and sense stuck energy, blockages, or tangled places. Then they comb them out with their fingers, pulling out anything that doesn't belong. End the combing with a fluffing, as if the aura was made of cotton.

A clean and solid grounding practice after an intense spiritual experience can also help prevent what I call *spiritual backlash*. Spiritual backlash could also be referred to as an energy hangover. If you've ever had a hangover from drinking alcohol you already have a pretty good idea of what spiritual backlash feels like. It comes from running a lot of energy and then not fully grounding that energy out, but carrying it with you. That energy needs to be burned off or released, otherwise you face backlash.

As with any type of spiritual working, there are also mundane, regular world activities that you can do to help prevent spiritual backlash.

◆ **Prepare:** Before stepping into any spiritual working, take the time to prep your body, mind, and spirit. Prep work will look different depending on the type of spell or ritual you are doing and how your body functions.

◆ **Drink Water:** Spiritual work is thirsty work. Stay hydrated before, during, and after ritual as much as possible.

◆ **Eat Something:** It doesn't have to be a full meal, but get a little food in your system after doing intense work. If you are fasting before a ritual, it is even more important that you eat once the rite is complete.

+ **Ground:** See above. Take some time to reconnect with the earth. This may include putting your hands on the ground and releasing any excess or pent up energy.

+ **Sleep:** Take a nap or commit to getting a full night's sleep after a major ritual working.

+ **Go Outside:** A little time in nature—even if that's a parking lot outside your building—can help shift your energy and bring you back to yourself.

CREATING SACRED SPACE

The creation of sacred space is the acknowledgment that we step from our mundane world, our regular life, into a ritual. We are not *making* a space sacred, but rather we are calling our attention to the sacredness that is already there. It is a process of us acknowledging the sacredness, not a creation of it.

It starts with casting a circle, creating an energy barrier between your ritual and the outside world. This is done for two reasons. The first reason is to protect your working. The barrier keeps your ritual contained until you want to release it. The second is to keep any entities out of your ritual space. Only you get to determine what entities are allowed in and a circle creates that barrier.

Traditionally, a circle is cast using an athame, a wand, or the first one or two fingers of your dominant hand. You use this tool to direct energy around your ritual space. At each direction (north, south, east, west, above, and below) a ward is created to help you lock in your circle. One of the ways to lock into your circle is to draw an invoking pentacle at each of the directions. However, once you are adept at casting circles, you can use other signs or symbols to lock in your energy.

The elements can be invited into your circle as you cast it or after you have created the energetic barrier. The order of this happening is up to you. Each ritual in this book has a slightly different process, matching the deity or entity that is being worked with.

The rituals included in this book are written from the perspective of someone in the northern hemisphere. Where it is common to cast a circle going deosil in the northern hemisphere, it is common to do the opposite in the southern hemisphere. The elements in the northern hemisphere are connected to the directions: earth = north, air = east, fire = south, water = west. In the south, these elemental/directional distinctions are not the same. There is some debate on the directional/elemental connections in the southern hemisphere.

THE "WORKING"

The working of the ritual is sometimes referred to as the meat (or tofu) of the ritual. Once sacred space is set, the working is what the ritual is all about. This may be trance, journey, devotional, spell work, or many other things. The ritual working may be a small and fast process or it may take hours.

RELEASING SACRED SPACE

The releasing of the ritual is done in the reverse order as the creating of sacred space.

GLOSSARY OF TERMS

Ascended Masters: Formerly embodied entities that have achieved spiritual enlightenment and help humans from their new plane of being. Jesus is thought to be an ascended master.

Athame: A ritual knife that is used to direct energy. Traditionally a double-sided blade. Many traditions have specific rules on the color of the hilt.

Banishing Pentacle: A specific way of drawing the pentacle, used to release energy or remove a barrier between this world and the next.

Book of Shadows: A journal or diary kept for all your magickal practices.

Coven: A group of Witches/Pagans that meet regularly to do ritual and magick together. Often these groups make a ritual commitment to each other.

Deosil: A clockwise movement.

God Pose: Standing up straight with your arms crossed across your chest. This pose resembles the pose that the dead are put in with their arms crossed over the chest.

Godd: A gender neutral term for polytheist use of "gods."

Goddess Pose: Standing up straight with your arms open and raised above your head. Your arms would resemble a V shape.

Evocation: Calling a spirit, being, entity into a ritual space.

Invocation: Calling a spirit, being entity, into the body of a priestess.

Invoking Pentacle: A specific way of drawing the pentacle, used to lock energy in or create a barrier between this world and the next.

Otherworld: The realms that are just next to and connected with our world, but which we typically can't see. The Otherworld could refer to the Fae realms, the realm of the ancestors, or the realm of the Godds.

Skyclad: Being naked, literally "clad with the sky only."

Smudge: To cleanse with smoke from burning herbs or resins.

Solitary: A Witch/Pagan that works alone without a coven or group.

Widdershins: A counter-clockwise movement.

Section One

DEVOTION

3

WORKING WITH DEITY

I believe something that is rather unpopular to the rest of the Pagan world. I believe that the Godds need us as much as we need them. We say that the Godds are immortal, but how do the Godds become immortal? Their immortality comes through our human mortality. We keep them going, we help them continue to live, at least on this plane of existence.

We Pagans and Witches tend to give pretty wide allowance for people to have their own spiritual experiences, to the point of creating a personal gnosis. At times these experiences and beliefs may actually go against proven history or practices from ancient times. Generally speaking, creating new practices is wonderful; new traditions and systems of worship hold the potential for magick and beauty. However, a personal experience needs to take historical context into consideration. Without looking at history and culture, we are completely making up systems, which in the very worst of cases may support unhealthy people, ego-driven practitioners, or even pathological liars. It has happened many times before in the history of modern Witchcraft.

Trust your personal experience with the Godds, but also know and understand their history. Let these two threads work together to develop a strong and solid practice with your personal spirits.

Working with deity can be a totally fulfilling and life-changing experience. A relationship with a divine being is an act of devotion. These connections may require you to believe the unbelievable. This bond may ask you to bow down to them with honor and respect. Being devoted to a Godd means that you remember that there are beings with more insight, experience, and knowledge than we, as humans, have. Devotion asks us to be humble, to listen, and to honor their insight.

However, devotion also means trusting ourselves and being willing to listen to our instincts. Devotion means saying no when things don't feel in alignment with our highest good. Working with divinity forces you to remember that your body and life are precious gifts. The Godds are not perfect beings and they do not fully comprehend the needs of the human body.

When I teach on this subject my mantra is *body trumps spirit*. This is the bottom line, no matter what. I encourage you to work with this mantra too. Always remember body trumps spirit. Trust your body to tell you what is right, what is working for you, and what is not okay. If it isn't okay with you—and for you—then don't do it.

GETTING TO KNOW A GODD

Deciding to work with a deity is just the first battle. Once things are set in motion you have to begin the building of a relationship. Think about what it takes to create a solid and trusting human relationship, because it isn't that different. It will take time and dedication for a relationship to unfold. The following steps can help you to develop and nurture a new relationship with a deity.

1. **Do Your Research:** I have said it before and I will say it again—you need to have some understanding of a Godd's origins, culture, and

historical story. This is just good spiritual manners. Get to know their history as you would get to know the history of a new lover.

2. **Check Your Place of Power:** Once you have made the decision to reach out to a specific Godd, go to your Place of Power and meet with them. From your PoP, all of the Godds, allies, and potential helpers are accessible. At the end of this section you will find a trance to help lead to you meeting these entities.

3. **Ask Other Practitioners:** Connect with other people that work with the same deities that you are interested in working with. Gaining insight and experience from other worshippers will deepen your connection to any Godd and give you important information that may not be gained from reading sources only.

4. **Do Ritual:** Rituals allow you to get out of your head and connect more deeply from a place of spirit. Do a ritual for your deities as an introduction to your personal spiritual nature. An introduction ritual is included at the end of this section.

5. **Create Sacred Space:** Make space for your deity in your home or garden. Create a shrine or place for devotion where you can spend time opening up to your Godd. This place can be as complex or simple as you'd like, but create it with the intention of it being a portal for you and your deity to commune and connect.

6. **Prayer:** Prayer doesn't have to look like being on your knees at the side of your bed with your hands folded together. Prayer is an offering to the Godds. Prayer is a conversation, a calling, a love song. When you pray you might sing a song of devotion, chant a mantra, or recite a poem to and for your Godd. It is an offering of your voice and an excellent way to connect to spirit.

7. **Take Your Time:** In order to fully get to know a new entity, focus solely on that relationship for a while. If you are drawn to working with a couple of different Godds, an ancestor, and a Fae being all at the same time, it is easy to get confused or conflate information. Give

yourself space for one new relationship at a time. This allows you to learn the nuance of that entity. You get used to their voice, their signs, their symbols. After you are clear on how it works with that one specific spirit it is easier to open up to other relationships. Too many new relationships at the same time can be confusing.

8. **Keep Notes:** Yes, highly unromantic, but that's what a Book of Shadows is all about, keeping track of our magickal working! I encourage the use of a *new* journal for specific Otherworld work. I don't just mean a separate journal for all your Otherworld work, but a specific journal for each of the entities that you work with. It might be overkill, but it totally works for me. If I am working with Brigid I can reflect on just the notes connected with her. I can read all the spells and rituals connected to her. It keeps things organized and much easier to look back on. I know that this could add up to a lot of journals, but it's worth it. Another totally unromantic suggestion is to use a three-ring binder for your Book of Shadows. I have a black three ring binder for my BoS that I've used since the age of fifteen. It's got all my cool notes and spells in it going back to early days. But I also put in binder tabs that help me to track and separate my work with specific entities.

THESE GODDS

The deities included in this book are all Godds that I have worked with in my own personal spiritual practice. Five of the Godds in this book (Dionysus, Brigid, Morgan LeFay, Baba Yaga, and Thor) are all from my "personal pantheon" and I work with them devotionally every day. In my personal practice, I have what I lovingly refer to as my "B Team" or the second string. These are the Godds that I know well. I call on them regularly, but they are not "mine." I am not devoted to working with them. Two of the Godds (Lilith and Aradia) in this book are from my personal B Team. Then I have the Godds I refer to as the "Others"; these are the deities that I know from a distance. I know their story, I know their energy, and I have had some interaction with them, but we aren't really close. You might think of these as my Godd acquaintances. The final two Godds (Hapi and Mithras) are a part of this group.

In writing this book, I spent a lot of time with each of these deities. We had conversations and I listened to how they wanted to be represented. I read many books, articles, and blogs, written by other Witches and occultists, learning how other folks are in relationship with these Godds. In some cases I was pleasantly surprised by my findings and in at least one case, my relationship with a Godd that I only knew as an acquaintance deepened into something more devotional.

With all the deities listed in this book you will find a bit of history, cultural context, and story. The stories are based on myth and legend, but all of the stories are written by me. Some deities' stories are so well known that the tales in this book may be familiar. If I wrote my version of Sleeping Beauty, you would still know that it was Sleeping Beauty, even in my words. In the cases where a legend or myth exists only in a fragment, snippet, or in the case of Mithras, a pictorial relief, I have completely written the tale based on my work with those Godds. With the fragments, I asked the Godds for their input and vision on how to best tell their story.

It is also important to remember that we are reading their stories and learning their myths with a modern lens. No matter how much we try, we will never be able to fully comprehend the world that these Godds were born into. It doesn't matter how much study we have done on a culture; that study was done with our modern lens and it will impact everything that we do.

Regionality is also an issue. We might think of the Greek Godds as belonging to all of Greece, but that's not really how it worked for the ancient people of Greece. Worship was much more regional. One city, town, or village would have their own way of doing things and potentially their own version of what we consider well-known Godds. The deity that we are familiar with, at this point in history, is a slightly different one than existed in ancient Athens.

Each deity section will also come with a ritual that you can do on your own or with a group to help deepen your connection to that Godd. These rituals can (and should) be adjusted and adapted to meet your needs. Beyond that, these rituals can (and should) be adapted to be used with other deities.

•—◆•◆•◆—•

MEETING A GODD IN YOUR
PLACE OF POWER

•—◆•◆•◆—•

Begin with the trance induction.

Open your inner eye, your Witch's eye, and see before you the door to your Place of Power. Take a moment to notice if there are any changes to the door since you last visited. Knock three times on the door, turn the handle, and walk into your Place of Power.

Find yourself at the center of your land. Take a moment to notice any changes since your last visit; anything that may have grown, been added, or shifted since you were here before. Listen for any noises and take a moment to take in the scent of this place. From the center of your place, state the name of the Godd you seek. Speak their name out loud in your place and then turn slowly in a circle, looking for a trail or path.

You will know when you see the trail or path that leads to this Godd. Once the path becomes clear, walk toward it. Take one step and then another, bringing yourself closer to the Godd that you seek. As you follow the path, take note of anything interesting or unusual along the way. Take note of any animals or plants that may be near. Take note of any sounds or smells. Pay attention with all your senses.

You come to a place where the Godd you seek resides. This place may be a simple clearing in the landscape, it may be a plain domicile, it could look like a grand temple space, or a large dramatic dwelling. Trust the images that come for the Godd you seek and allow yourself to explore the landscape here in their space. (Pause)

The Godd you seek appears before you. Give yourself some time to ask them the questions that you hold. (Pause)

Ask this deity if they are willing to work with you and step into relationship. (Pause)

Ask this Godd what they most want from you as a sign of your newly forged relationship. (Pause)

Ask this deity for a symbol or token so that you will know when you encounter them and not an imposter. (Pause)

Remember that your time in this place is limited, but you can return here anytime you need to. For now, offer your gratitude to this Godd and say your goodbyes. Return to the path that brought you here and follow the path back out to the center of your Place of Power. In the center, find your door, easily open it, and step back through, closing the door behind you.

Close your inner Witch's eye. Notice your breath in your physical body. Slowly open your normal seeing eyes and allow yourself to fully come back into your body. Pat your edges, touch the top of your head, and say your name out loud three times.

Take a moment to drink a glass of water and write down the important parts of your journey. Make sure to note anything the Godd said to you that you will need to remember for future encounters with them.

PORTAL TRANCE

This exercise should be done when you have a sign, symbol, or question that you are seeking verification or deeper information on.

Begin with the trance induction.

Open your Witch's inner eye and see before you a spiral staircase going down. Place a foot on the first step and begin to follow the stairs down. Step by step, let your feet carry you down the stairs. Take note as you move downward what substance your staircase is made of. As you move further down, notice anything interesting or curious in and around your staircase. Let your feet carry you step by step, further and further down.

The stairs spiral around as you move down, down, down, getting ever closer to the bottom. Putting one foot in front of the other, take one step down and the next step down. As you spiral around, see the bottom of the staircase and a door in front of you.

Take note of this door, as it is a door that will help you discover answers. What is this door made of? What color is it? What substance is the handle made from? Take in all of the details of this door.

When you feel ready, draw the sign, symbol, or question on the door with your finger. Allow the symbol, sign, or words to glow as you use your finger to draw them. When complete, knock on the door three times and turn the handle.

Inside the door you will be shown information and insight on what was written on the door. Take time to explore this answer. (Long pause) When you have all of the information you can take in for now, step back through the doorway. Close the door and begin to walk back up the steps that brought you to this portal.

Step up, one foot in front of the other, taking the steps up, up, up. Let the steps move you upward, one foot after another, back up the stairs. As you reach the top of the staircase, step back into your body. Breathe deeply and slowly, allowing all of yourself to reconnect to your body. Slowly open your eyes, tap the edges of your body, and say your name out loud three times.

—◆•◆•◆—

MEETING A GODD RITUAL

—◆•◆•◆—

This ritual is intended to be done as a solitary practitioner. It is for you to connect with a specific deity. However, the ritual can be modified if a group or coven wants to meet with the same Godd all at once. Set aside at least an hour when you will be undisturbed. You will need to have already done research on your Godd in order to know what items, foods, and offerings they would want in their sacred space.

SUPPLIES

two white candles

incense

athame or wand

bowl of salt water

statue or image of deity

fresh flowers

food offering

drink offering

quartz crystal

SET UP

You will need the following items already set up on your altar: two white candles, incense that would be pleasing to your deity (or frankincense), your athame or wand, and a small bowl of salt water. Have the following items available, but not set up on the altar (you will set them up during the ritual): a statue or image of the deity you are calling upon, fresh flowers that they would like, foods and drink that they would like, and a quartz crystal that will comfortably fit in your pocket. Keep your journal close by and take down notes anytime something happens that you want to keep track of.

RITUAL

Begin by centering yourself. Take some deep breaths and draw in all of your parts, focus on calling yourself back into your body. Breathe deeply and with intention. Place your hands on your center and allow yourself to be fully you, present, in the moment, and ready to step into magickal space.

Take the bowl of salt water and sprinkle the water around your ritual circle. Focus on clearing this space, making it ready for the ritual you are beginning. Light the incense and walk the smoke around your ritual space, focusing on charging your circle as you move through the area.

Using your wand or athame, face the north. Draw an invoking pentacle in front of you and say the following:

By the Earth that is my body, I cast this
circle in strength and power.

Turn and face the east, draw an invoking pentacle, and say the following:

By the Air that is my breath, I cast this
circle in knowledge and understanding.

Turn and face the south, draw an invoking pentacle, and say the following:

By the Fire of my bright spirit, I cast this
circle in energy and connection.

Turn and face the west, draw an invoking pentacle, and say the following:

By the Water of my living blood, I cast this
circle in trust and emotion.

Return to the north and draw another invoking pentacle to seal the circle that you have created. Stand in the center of your space and draw an invoking pentacle above you, visualizing closing the circle up and above your head. Say the following:

By all that is above, I cast this
circle in mystery and faith.

Point your tool to the ground, draw an invoking pentacle, and say the following:

By all that is below, I cast this
circle in depth and wisdom.

Return the wand or athame to your altar.
Say this:

The circle is cast, I am between the worlds,
and what happens between the worlds
changes all the worlds. So mote it be.

Light the white candles.

Speak your intention into the circle. Call out the name of the deity that you want to work with. Speak out loud what you know about them and why you want them to join your ritual. As you speak, feel their energy coming into your circle. Speak from the heart and don't worry about the words being right. Say what you feel called to say. Welcome them to the ritual. If you find yourself struggling with what to say, start with the following and then fill in your own words.

> *I call on (name of deity) to join me in my circle to-*
> *day. I call upon you in devotion. I (state your name)*
> *humbly call upon you (name of deity) to help me*
> *with your wisdom and power. Be here now.*

Follow this with your own words of acknowledgment and devotion; explain why you want to connect with this Godd.

Give yourself a moment to notice any shifts or changes in the space.

Sprinkle the statue or image of your Godd with salt water and run the statue through the smoke of the incense. Place the statue between the two white candles on your altar. Say the following:

> *Come (name of deity) and reside in this space.*
> *You are welcome here Great One. In this*
> *space you are honored.*

Place the flowers on the altar. Say the following:

> *Please accept this offering (name of deity). These*
> *flowers are a symbol of my devotion to you.*

Place the food and drink on the altar. Say the following:

> *Please accept this offering (name of deity). This food*
> *and drink is a symbol of my devotion to you.*

Place the quartz crystal at the base of the statue. Say the following:

> *I call upon you (name of deity) to charge this crystal*
> *with your spirit and your blessing. I ask this boon so*
> *that I may carry you with me. I ask in devotion*
> *and in desire to develop relationship with you.*

Sit in devotion. Allow some time to pass. During this time you may want to chant, sing, or silently meditate in devotion to your Godd. Write down anything interesting or important that happens. This includes any seemingly random thoughts that may pop into your head during this time. When you feel complete in this process, move on to closing the ritual.

Hold up the charged quartz crystal and say the following:

> *Thank you Great One. Thank you (name*
> *of deity) for being in circle with me today,*
> *thank you for your blessing.*

Kiss the crystal and place it back on the altar. When the circle is open, keep it with you, in your pocket or in your bra.

Offer a thank you to your deity, speaking from your heart. Express your gratitude to this Godd for joining you and let them know they are welcome in this space that you have created going forward.

Pick up your wand or athame and point it to the ground. Draw the banishing pentacle and say the following:

> *By the deep below, I release this circle.*

Point your wand to the sky, draw the banishing pentacle, and say the following:

> *By the great above, I release this circle.*

Face the north, draw the banishing pentacle, and say the following:

> *By the Earth that is my body, I release this circle.*

Face the west, draw the banishing pentacle, and say the following:

By the Water of my blood, I release this circle.

Face the south, draw the banishing pentacle, and say the following:

By the Fire of my bright spirit, I release this circle.

Face the east, draw the banishing pentacle, and say the following:

By the Air that is my breath, I release this circle.

Return to facing the north and draw the banishing pentacle for a final time. Say the following:

*The circle is open, but unbroken; may the
piece of (name of deity) go in my heart.*

Put out the candles and incense, and place the crystal in your pocket. Use this crystal any time that you want to feel connected to this deity. It can be placed on their altar any time you may feel that it needs a charge up from their energy.

4

DEITIES OF
MAGICK

One might argue that all Godds are deities of magick, and I would agree with that, but there are some deities that can take you deeper into magick, deeper into your personal power, deeper into conjuring spells for transformation. These Godds are often found on the fringes. They live on the edges of the societies they were born into. Their abilities, skills, and powers are outside of what is held in the mainstream cultures. They know how to bend and manipulate and work the powers that are around them.

Connecting to Godds of magick can be challenging. These Godds may test your mettle. These Godds may have expectations and you will need to meet them. These Godds will ask you to grow, often in ways that are uncomfortable.

The Godds of magick included in this book are deities whose worship never fully died out. Although they may have been transformed into legends, folktales, or Catholic saints, they survived. The ability to survive is also part of their magick.

BABA YAGA

BABA YAGA HISTORY

Baba Yaga is the old woman who lives in the woods. She is the Witch who entices Hansel and Gretel. She is the stuff of legends used to frighten small children and keep them from wandering in the woods alone. She is cranky and impatient. Baba Yaga will just as likely eat you as offer you any help.

Baba Yaga comes from Eastern Europe and Russia, where modern folk still tell her tales. Her power has never disappeared from that part of the world. The first known written reference of Baba Yaga is from a book written in 1755, called *Rossijskaya Grammatika* (Russian Grammar). Part of this book is a reference list of Slavic Gods and what would have been their Roman counterparts. Baba Yaga is listed in the text with no Roman counterpart.

This Goddess is a single entity and she is also more than that. One of the meanings of *Baba* is actually a title, an honorific for an older woman. *Babushka* is the name for grandmother or old woman in Russian, which is often shortened to *Baba* as a term of endearment. There could be many Babas that roam and rule the dark woods of Russia and Eastern Europe. Tracing her name back further, we can find that it may have originally meant sorceress.

She is not a beloved character in history or in modern times. She is feared because of her age, because of her power, because she lives alone in the woods. Baba Yaga is not good or bad, she just is.

Her stories live on in folktales. There are a cast of characters and helpers that appear in many of these tales. One of these characters is a man named Ivan, who is often described as a poor bumbling fool or a wealthy man with no common sense. Over and over he is confronted by Baba Yaga and set to a series of tasks in order to prove he is worthy of her help. A firebird shows up in many of her tales. It is said to bring knowledge or sight to the one that is able to capture just one of its feathers. Baba also has three lovers: a white rider on a white horse that represents the dawn, a red rider on a red horse the represents the day, and a black rider on a black horse that represents the night.

There is a cat that lives in her hut. He often helps those that seek out Baba Yaga by giving them hints or helpful information on how to succeed in her challenges. There is a pair of disembodied hands that do her bidding. A frog, a mouse, a herder, sisters, and a musical horn are all things that show up in different tales featuring Baba Yaga.

Baba Yaga lives in a house that walks on chicken feet. Her home is surrounded by a fence with flaming skulls on each post. She flies through the air on her mortar and pestle, cackling and steering with her broom. She holds so many roles in her culture of origin, being seen as cloud, moon, winter, and death, but also as Earth Goddess, protector of women and children, initiator, and ancestor.

Call on Baba Yaga when you need help making decisions. She brings clarity and insight, not telling us what to choose, but helping us to make space for a clear decision to come forward. Baba Yaga can help you open to your own magick more deeply. She is the mystic in the woods, connected to the forces of nature, and she can teach you how to maintain those connections too.

No matter the story, Baba Yaga is an initiator. When you step into her realm, you leave changed. When you approach this powerful grandmother, you leave what no longer serves you behind and step into something new.

HER STORY

There was once a small young girl named Vasalisa. Her mother was very ill, and as she lay on her deathbed she called her lovely daughter to her side. The mother took her daughter's hand and placed a small doll in her palm. "She will be your guide," the mother said. "She will always help you. She is a mother's blessing."

A couple of years after her mother's death, Vasalisa's father married another woman who had two daughters of her own. The father was often away, and while he was gone Vasalisa's stepmother and stepsisters were very cruel to her. They made her cook all the food. They forced her to do all the cleaning, the sewing, and the gardening. Vasalisa worked very hard to make her family happy, but no matter what she did, their cruelty continued.

One morning, Vasalisa's stepmother conspired to get rid of her stepdaughter once and for all. She put out all of the fires in the house and told Vasalisa that she must go into the woods to find Baba Yaga and get fire for the house. Vasalisa had no choice but to agree.

The young girl bravely and boldly entered the forest with her dolly in her pocket. She had no idea how to find Baba Yaga or how to get fire, but she began her journey following a path deeper and deeper into the cover of the trees.

She came to a fork in the road, unsure of which path to take. Vasalisa put her hand into her pocket and squeezed her dolly. The little dolly gave a gentle tug to the right side of her hand and Vasalisa followed the path in that direction.

This same thing happened over and over again. Vasalisa would come to a fork in the road, and unsure, she would reach into her pocket for the guidance of her dolly. Her uncertainty would boil over and then, every time, her dolly would tug on her hand, directing her on which path to follow.

Eventually she came to a clearing in the trees. In the clearing, a fence of flaming skulls surrounded a small hut strutting around on chicken feet. Vasalisa peered out from the cover of the trees, watching the odd little house moving its way around the yard.

From above she heard a swoosh, a crack, and a cackle. An old bony woman was riding in a mortar and pestle across the night sky using a broom like a rudder. She swirled in a circle, coming ever closer to the hut. With a thump and a thud the old crone landed in the yard, hopping out of her mortar and stomping into her chicken footed hut.

Cautiously, Vasalisa came out from the cover of the forest, boldly walking through the gate of flaming skulls, and knocked on the door of the hut. Baba Yaga yanked open the door, peering down at the child. Her smile revealing a terrifying row of sharpened teeth.

"Please grandmother," Vasalisa says, "I need fire to help my family."

When the word grandmother escaped the young girl's mouth, Baba Yaga's eyes grew wide. The old crone pulled open the door wider and gestured for the girl to enter.

"I will help you," sniffed Baba Yaga as she closed the door. "But first you must complete some tasks for me, and if you fail, I will eat you."

Baba Yaga told Vasalisa that she must clean the house, cook dinner enough to fill the table, and sort all of the good grain from the ruined grain in the yard. If she was able to complete all of these tasks before sunrise Baba Yaga would let her live another night. After issuing this decree, Baba Yaga flew off on her mortar and pestle, leaving Vasalisa to sort.

Vasalisa cooked the food and cleaned the house. As the night drew on she began to sort the grain, but quickly realized it was truly an impossible task. She began to cry, pulling out her dolly for comfort. The dolly pet her hand and told her to not to worry, to rest her weary head, and trust that all would be well in the morning.

When the dawn arrived Baba Yaga returned to the chicken footed hut. She saw the girl had completed the tasks and with a huff, Baba Yaga sat down at the table and devoured every crumb of food. Clearly the crone was irritated, but Vasalisa remained quiet as the old woman hungrily ate.

As the day wore on toward night, Baba Yaga gave Vasalisa another set of tasks. The young girl was told to clean the house, cook dinner enough to fill the table, and sort the pile of dirt and poppy seeds out in the yard. Again, Baba Yaga flew away into the night and Vasalisa was left alone to complete her work.

Vasalisa cooked the food and cleaned the house. Again, as the night drew on she began to sort the dirt from the poppy seeds, but quickly realized this was truly an impossible task. She began to cry and reached for her dolly. The dolly told her not to worry, to rest her weary head, and trust that all would be well in the morning.

When the morning came, Baba Yaga returned to the hut and saw that, once again, all the tasks had been completed. The crone was clearly upset. Rather than sitting down to eat, she leaned in closely to the young girl. Vasalisa could feel the old woman's hot breath on her face. Baba Yaga eyeballed the girl closely, smacking her lips and squinting her eyes. Baba Yaga asked, "How did you come to complete these tasks, girl?" and pointed a bony finger into the girl's chest as she spoke.

Vasalisa paused, her heart racing, while searching for the right answer. She knew that the threat of being eaten was no more dangerous than in that moment. Finally, Vasalisa responded, "From the blessings of my mother."

"Blessings?!" Baba Yaga screeched. "We will have no blessings here!" The crone stalked out of the house, dragging the girl along with her toward the fence line of skulls. She took one of the glowing skulls in her bony hands and pushed it into Vasalisa arms. "Be gone, wretched child!" Baba Yaga spat.

Vasalisa wasted no time. She took the glowing skull and ran into the forest as fast as she could. This time when she came to a fork in the road, the skull directed her which way to go. She kept running as if Baba Yaga was nipping at her heels, not stopping until she finally reached the safety of her house. Inside the house her stepmother and stepsisters still waited in the cold and dark without fire.

When Vasalisa entered the house, the skull turned its focus, putting its glowing eyes on the family members huddled together. With a flash the fire sparked, incinerating the family. Vasalisa took over running the household, now master of her domain.

BABA YAGA CORRESPONDENCES

- Mortar and Pestle

- Cat

- Firebird

- Chicken

- Frog

- Mouse

- Musical Horn

BABA YAGA RITUAL:
THE SORTING CHALLENGE

One of the challenges that Baba Yaga gives to her unsuspecting visitors is a series of impossible tasks often involving sorting. Baba Yaga threatens those who seek her wisdom with death if they are unable to sort. We may find ourselves in situations when we are out of sorts or unable to make a decision. It can sometimes be impossible to know what stays in and what needs to be released. It is moments like these when I call upon Baba Yaga for help. It is through the completion of impossible tasks that we come closer to the truth of a situation. It is through the sorting of what belongs and what doesn't that we might make a better decision. Sacred sorting gives us the opportunity to connect to Baba Yaga's wisdom and better see the best course of action.

This ritual is written for a solitary practitioner looking for clarity and help with decision-making and discernment. It can easily be modified for a group or coven. If working with a coven, make a larger batch of sorting items (see below).

SUPPLIES

one white candle

one red candle

one black candle

bowl of salt water

mortar and pestle

statue or image of Baba Yaga

small white candle

athame

vodka

offering cup

items for sorting

bowl to hold items

SET UP

On your altar space, place: one white candle, one red candle, one black candle. In front of the candles place a statue or image of Baba Yaga. Next to the statue put the offering cup. In front of the statue, place a bowl of salt water, a mortar and pestle, and a small white candle for Baba Yaga. Near your altar keep the vodka and the bowl with items to sort.

Gather together a pot of items to sort. I have a perpetual cauldron of what I call "Baba's beans," which is a mixture of red beans, lentils, dried corn, some sea glass, golden marbles, matches, black beans, and some other bits that have made it into the mix over the years. Make your mix out what whatever feels appropriate, but small items about the size of a bean are ideal. Mix these items together and put them in a cauldron or large bowl.

RITUAL

Ground and center yourself. Do what you need to do in order to bring yourself into full presence. Breathe deeply. When you feel ready, pick up your athame.

Turn and face the north. With your athame, draw an invoking pentacle in front of you, creating a lock in your circle, and then say:

> *I call upon the north, the energy of the Earth. I call*
> *upon the mystery of the ancestors and the Witches in*
> *the woods. I call upon the knowing that lives in my*
> *bones. I call the north and welcome Earth.*

Using your athame, trace a circle around you while you turn to the east. Draw an invoking pentacle in front of you, creating a lock in your circle, and then say:

> *I call upon the east, the energy of the Air. I call*
> *upon sound, song, and breath. I call upon the*
> *wild one flying through the sky. I call upon the*
> *words of blessings that live on my tongue.*
> *I call the east and welcome Air.*

Use your athame to continue the circle, drawing it deosil around you as you face the south. Draw an invoking pentacle in front of you, creating a lock in your circle, and then say:

> *I call upon the south, the energy of the Fire.*
> *I call upon the spark of knowing and the magick*
> *of the flame. I call upon the heat of my passion.*
> *I call the south and welcome Fire.*

Again, use your athame to continue the circle, drawing that bubble around you as you face the west. Draw an invoking pentacle in front of you, creating a lock in your circle, and then say:

> *I call upon the west, the energy of Water. I*
> *call upon the depths, the emotions, and the*
> *wisdom of my blood. I call upon the water,*
> *the tears, and the flow. I call upon my knowing.*
> *I call the west and welcome Water.*

Turn again to the north, completing your circle, and draw another invoking pentacle in front of you. Raise your athame to the top of your circle, drawing a lock for the above, and say:

> *By all that flies above.*

Lower your athame to the ground, drawing a final lock for the below, and say:

> *By all that crawls below. The circle*
> *is cast. So mote it be.*

Light the white candle and say:

> *For the Dawn.*

Light the red candle and say:

> *For the Day.*

Light the black candle and say:

> *For the Night. Hail the Three Riders.*

Face your altar, pour some vodka for Baba Yaga, and say:

> *I call to you Baba Yaga. Wild Witch of the woods.*
> *Wise one. Bone mother, seer, Witch. I call to you*
> *and invite you into my circle. I ask for your guidance*
> *and wisdom. I ask for your help and clarity in sorting*
> *through what needs cleaning up and clearing away.*
> *Baba Yaga, I invite you into this ritual to lend your*
> *energy and guidance. Hail and welcome Baba Yaga.*

Place your hands over the bowl of mixed items and state out loud the things that you need help with untangling, sorting, or clearing out. Speak from your heart, allowing all of the places where you feel trapped to be sent into the mixture. You may find yourself getting emotional. Allow whatever is coming through to come. Let out the anger, sadness, or frustration. Release it all out into the mixture.

Rinse your hands off in the bowl of salt water, allowing any last vestiges of what you were putting in the mixture to be cleansed off of you.

Begin sorting. Work your way through the mixture, separating all of the parts and pieces into their own groups. Don't try to analyze this process, just be in it and sort piece from piece. You may want to stop the sorting process before you have worked through the whole bowl, but keep going, sort through the entire bowl.

When you have finished sorting, take a look at the piles you have created. What needs to go and what stays? What is worthy to keep? What is it time to let go of? Light the white candle for Baba Yaga and take time to journal and speak out loud to her. Share with her what has become clear to you through the sorting. If there is anything left to untangle, set this out in front of Baba Yaga and ask for her aid and assistance.

When you feel complete, speak your gratitude from your heart to Baba Yaga. Then say:

> Thank you, Baba Yaga, wild Witch of the woods.
> Thank you wise one, bone mother, seer, Witch.
> Thank you for joining in my circle. Thank you for
> bringing forth your knowledge and wisdom.
> From this circle I bid you hail and farewell.

Extinguish the black, red, and white candles and say:

> Goodnight, Good-day, Good-dawn.
> Hail and farewell, Three Riders.

Release your circle by picking up your athame and unlocking the pentacles that you placed below you, followed by the pentacle above you. Turn to the north, point your athame outwards, and cut through the circle you built. Turn to the west and say:

> *Thank you to the Water. Thank you to the depths,*
> *the emotions, and the wisdom of my blood.*
> *Hail and farewell, Water.*

Release the pentacle and turn to the south. Face the south, cutting through the circle you built as you turn. Say:

> *Thank you Fire. Thank you spark of knowing, and*
> *magick of the flame. Hail and farewell, Fire.*

Release this pentacle and turn to the east. Face the east, cutting through the circle as you turn. Say:

> *Thank you Air. Thank you sound, song,*
> *and breath. Hail and farewell, Air.*

Release the pentacle you built and turn to the north. Face the north and say:

> *Thank you Earth. Thank you, ancestors and*
> *Witches in the woods. Hail and farewell, Earth.*

Release the pentacle, return your blade to your altar, and clap your hands three times. Gather up your sorted items. They should be released into the world. Take them to a crossroads and dispose of them, pour them into running water, like a stream or river, or shake them loose in a wild place. Just make sure all pieces are biodegradable. The work is done, Hail Baba Yaga.

BRIGID

BRIGID HISTORY

The Goddess Brigid comes from the Celtic diaspora, with a close connection to Ireland. She was such a potent force of magick for the Irish people that, even with the conversion to Christianity, they were unable to stop people from honoring her. Her story morphed and changed over time and her title became that of a saint. Because of this transformation, Brigid is still honored in Ireland today.

It is important to remember, as we look at this Goddess with our modern lens, that she was not just one thing to this wide swath of people. The small tribes and villages of Ireland are quite large, and the greater Celtic diaspora even larger. Brigid was many different Goddesses, spirits, entities, Fae-beings, and Spirits of the Land that were all syncretized over time. All of these spirits from different local stories and folktales were compressed into a single mythological being: a Goddess. This is true for many of the ancient Godds, but it is especially true for Brigid. It is one explanation for her possessing such wide and varying skills and traits.

The Celtic system looks at the elements as a tri-fold power, and Brigid had relationship with all of them. The first element is land. Brigid connects to land in her role as the blacksmith. The second element is sea. Brigid is connected to the sea as a healer and midwife. Finally the third element is the sky. Here we see Brigid as the poet and orator, possessing the gifts of language.

Her name is found all over the landscape of the Celtic lands. Many of the tallest hills are called Brigid, Bride, Brida—but not just the high places; the rivers also possess her name. There are rivers all over the lands of the Celtic diaspora that bear her name, even showing up in places where the Irish settled in the United States.

In her story as Saint Brigid, the tales shift a bit. Rather than possessing the skills of all the realms, she is reduced to the daughter of a Druid. She is the last of her kind, the last of the old ways, but she turns away from her Druidic blood and birthright to devote herself to the Catholic faith. However, she retains the skill and knowledge of healing and the herbs of the land because of her Druid upbringing.

Over and over again in her stories we see her connected to fire and water, but it goes beyond that too. She can also be seen as the Goddess of birth and death. Many Pagans know Brigid as the midwife, and we think of the midwife as helping babies to be born, but this is only one half of the tale. Midwives also help the dead cross over, and Brigid was the first Goddess to keen over death, giving her the distinct connection to both the beginning and the end of life.

The Ulster Cycle is a collection of Irish legends and myths in which Brigid is mentioned as having three aspects, sometimes considered three sisters. There is Brigid the hospitaller, who takes care of those who travel, who takes care of the home, and keeps families safe. There is Brigid of judgments; she is the one who hears the court cases and makes fair judgments. And there is Brigid of the cowless, who watches over those who were soldiers and warriors and therefore have no lands.

There are many stories of Brigid, but all of these come to us after the transition into Christianity. Much of what we know of her from before is lost to time.

HER STORY

The ancient ones had many conflicts and there were many tribes whose anger with each other went deep and long into the past. One of these families was the Tuatha de Danann (pronounced: *too-uh-huh-dey-dah-nah*) and Brigid was a daughter of this tribe. Another family was the Fomorians (pronounced: *for-mawr-ee-uhn*) and Bres was a son of this tribe. As these things happen, Brigid and Bres fell in love and married with a hope that their union would bring peace to the land.

Although their marriage brought forth a beloved son, named Ruadan (pronounced: *roo-a-dawn*), there was still much unrest between the tribes. Ruadan was sent by the Tuatha De Danann to spy on the Fomorians and discover what it was they were up to. He was directed to find out all the details about their plotting and return that information to the leaders of the Tuatha De Danann.

Ruadan discovered the Fomorians had set the great blacksmith Goibniu (pronounced: *gov-nyoo*) to the task of making powerful magickal tools. When the young man reported this information back to the Tuatha De Danann, the elders sent him back into the camp of the Fomorians with instructions that he must kill Goibniu and stop them from creating these magickal weapons.

Ruadan was gifted with gab, like his mother Brigid, who could sing the stars down from the skies. One afternoon, in front of all of the leaders of the Fomorians, Ruadan went to the great blacksmith Goibniu and began to lather him with compliments. Ruadan spoke of Goibniu's many gifts and talents. The young one sang his praises and filled his head with compliments and tales of valor that warriors of the future would tell because of the power of Goibniu's magickal weapons. As he used his silver tongued words and poetry, he begged of Goibniu to let him use a spear of his crafting. The blacksmith, so flattered by the words of the youth, proudly granted the request.

Immediately, Ruadan threw the spear at the blacksmith, hitting the great hulk of a man, but he missed his mark. Goibniu was only wounded, and the smith was fast and strong. He easily pulled out the spear and turned the tables on the young spy. He flipped the spear in his massive hand, angrily tossing the spear back at the son of Brigid. Ruadan died instantly.

Brigid was among the Fomorians with her husband as this took place. She watched as the spear pierced the body of her only child. She ran to her son and for the first time in the history of Ireland a keening was heard across the land. Brigid bewailed her son. She screamed his name and raised her tear-stained face to the heavens. She sobbed and cried and wailed. Brigid keened for her only son.

The spirit of her son lingered, watching his mother cry out, and Brigid could see him. Brigid saw his shape, his ethereal form, his specter, and knew that as much as it hurt, he needed to cross over to the realm of the ancestors. Calling upon her skills as midwife, she helped to open the gates.

The gates that she held open so many times before to bring new life into the world, she new held open to help her only son cross back into the land of the ancestors. Ruadan's spirit knew just what to do when the gate opened up.

Brigid keened one last time as her beautiful son's spirit went through the gates and she allowed them to close behind him.

BRIGID CORRESPONDENCES

- Blackberry
- Wells
- Forges
- Poetry
- Music
- Song
- Healing Herbs

———◆•◆•◆———

BRIGID RITUAL: TRANCE TO HER THREE FACES

———◆•◆•◆———

As a Goddess of land, sea, and sky, Brigid has her hands in many magickal pots. She can help you create new tools, birth something into life, and speak or sing your truth. Her power, her magick, is all-encompassing. Brigid can be called on at any time for virtually any reason.

SUPPLIES

blue candle

bowl of water

bowl of soil

incense

athame

statue or image of Brigid

SET UP

This ritual is written for one person, but can be modified for a group or coven. There is a trance included in this ritual. If you are doing the ritual on your own, record the trance ahead of time. If you are doing this ritual with a group, either have one person read the trance or record it so everyone can go on the journey at the same time.

Create an altar in a place where you will be undisturbed and able to lie down. On the altar, place a blue candle, a bowl of water, a bowl of soil, some incense, an athame, and a statue or image of Brigid. Have your journal, a pen, and a glass of water nearby.

RITUAL

Ground and center, allowing yourself to be fully present and ready for magickal working. Pick up your athame and draw a circle of blue fire around your space. Start in the east, turning in a full circle, sending blue fire through your body and out your athame, directing it around you. End in the east and then focus your directing energy above you and then below you, surrounding yourself in a sphere of blue fire.

With your athame in your dominant hand, pick up the bowl of soil. Turn and face the space between the west and north. Hold the bowl of soil above you while you draw an invoking pentacle with your athame, and say this:

I call upon the spirit of land. I call upon strength
and foundation. Hail and welcome, land.

Set down the bowl of soil and pick up the bowl of water. Turn to face the space between the south and the west. Hold the bowl of water above you, draw an invoking pentacle with your athame, and say this:

I call upon the spirit of sea. I call upon wisdom
and healing. Hail and welcome, sea.

Set down the bowl of water and light the incense, holding it above you. Face the east, holding the incense above you, and say this:

I call upon the spirit of sky. I call upon poetry
and clarity. Hail and welcome, sky.

Set down the incense and your athame. Light the blue candle and say this:

Brigid, Goddess of the forge, Goddess of healing,
Goddess of poetry, I invite you into my circle.
I call upon you, great lady, to bring your insight
and gifts to help guide my way. Brigid, I call
upon you in the spirit of devotion. Please join
me in this rite. Hail and welcome, Brigid.

Allow yourself to get comfortable and begin the trance, starting with the trance intro.

TRANCE

Before you is the door to your Place of Power. Knock three times, turn the handle, and step through into the center of your Place of Power. Take a moment to survey the area around you. Hold the intention of visiting with Brigid. Scan the land around you, taking time to notice a new path that stands out to you, calling you to follow it. Let your feet carry you forward, one foot in front of the other, following the path. Take note as you walk; what else do you see, smell, or hear along the path to Brigid's house.

Follow the path around a gentle bend. As the path straightens out you see a cottage nestled in a grove of trees. Continue to follow the path step by step until you can see the details of the house. The cottage appears simple and small from the outside, but it also appears to shimmer as if touched by magick. Next to the house is a beautiful, lush garden, where the plants seem to be in fruit and blossom at the same time. There is a hum of bees and birds and you can smell the freshness of ripe fruit.

On the other side of the house is a small shack, and through the open door you can see a fully-working forge. There is a faint smell of burning wood and melting iron in the air. You can see the tools of the blacksmith hanging on the back of the wall.

Stand before the house and notice where you feel called; which face of Brigid do you need to see right now in this moment? (Pause) Let yourself move either into the garden to meet with Brigid the midwife and healer, into the forge to meet with Brigid the blacksmith, or into the cottage to meet with Brigid the poet. (Pause) Move to that place and encounter the Goddess. Take time to speak with her. (Long pause)

Remember that your time for this visit is limited, but this place is available for you to return to at any point. Take a moment to ask any last questions, to express your gratitude, and say goodbye. (Pause) Leave the area of the cottage where you have visited with Brigid and return to the path that brought you here. Let your feet follow the path back, taking one step and then another.

The path leads you back to the center of your Place of Power. Step back through the door and close your inner eye from this place. Shift your awareness back to your physical body. Breathe, noticing the edges of your body, and slowly open your normal seeing eyes. Pat your edges and say your name out loud three times.

Take a moment to write down your experience and drink a glass of water.

When ready, step up to your altar and say this:

> *Brigid, triple Goddess of land, sea, and sky,*
> *thank you for being present in this ritual. I am*
> *grateful for your wisdom. I am grateful for*
> *your energy. Hail and farewell, Brigid.*

Snuff out the blue candle, pick up your athame in your dominant hand and the incense in the other. Face the east, draw the banishing pentacle, and say this:

> *Thank you, spirit of sky. Thank you for your gifts*
> *of poetry and clarity. Hail and farewell, sky.*

Snuff the incense and pick up the bowl of water. Face the space between south and west, draw the banishing pentacle, and say this:

> *Thank you spirit of sea. Thank you for your*
> *wisdom and healing. Hail and farewell, sea.*

Set down the bowl of water and pick up the bowl of soil. Turn to face the space between west and north, draw a banishing pentacle and say this:

> *Thank you spirit of land. Thank you for your*
> *strength and foundation. Hail and farewell, land.*

Set down the bowl of soil. Release the circle of blue flame that you created around you. Begin with the below and the above, using the athame to cut through the boundary. Use your athame to cut through the blue fire circle that surrounds you, releasing that boundary. Say this:

> *The circle is open, but unbroken. Hail and farewell.*

The work is done. Hail Brigid!

MORGAN LEFAY

MORGAN LEFAY HISTORY

I've had arguments with folks on whether Morgan LeFay is actually a Goddess. Here is my reasoning for why she is. Morgan LeFay, also known as Morgainne, Morgane, and occasionally Morgause, is a Witch and priestess from the Arthurian Legends. These tales were made popular in the romance period of Europe.

In 1485, a Frenchman named Thomas Mallory wrote a retelling of the story that he learned while traveling through the British Isles, called *Morte d'Arthur*. The characters he wrote about have older origins that go back hundreds of years to the Mabinogion, which is a collection of Welsh stories. Arthur features prominently in these tales and they are likely of an older oral tradition.

Tales of the High Priestess of Avalon or the Witch that was Arthur's sister, aunt, or other family member is repeated in stories over and over again. But just for a moment, let's pretend that there is nothing older written about Morgan LeFay than 1485. For more than 500 years people have been hearing the story of Morgan LeFay. She has been feared, worshipped, and believed to have magickal powers all this time. She is known for her magickal gifts, her understanding of herbs, and her connection to the Otherworld.

All the Godds were born at one point or another. Some of their births are connected to sacred spaces where they may have been a tutelary spirit. Some of their births are connected to a specific ancestor who did great acts and became immortalized after death. And some are the stuff of legends, with origins we could never even guess. Some of the deities that we love and worship were fictional characters. We give them power, we lift them up, we make them Godds. Morgan LeFay is a Goddess because we believe her to be one. This is the heart of what is remembered lives.

So, whether Morgan LeFay is an old Godd of mystical origins, an ancestor Witch, a tutelary spirit, or a completely fictional character, she has been believed in and worshipped for at least six hundred years. That's not too shabby.

Morgan LeFay is NOT the Morrigan of Irish myth. They are totally different creatures with a totally different energy. Morgan LeFay is also referred to as the Faerie Queen. This may be connected to her holding a ruling thumb over Avalon, which is seen as the Otherworld—the realm of the Fae. She understands how to travel back and forth between different realms. She is described as a shape-shifter and healer. She possesses many of the skills and talents that the Fae beings of ancient legends would have held. Does this make her Fae or Goddess? For me, the answer is yes—both.

Morgan LeFay is a Witch, a priestess, and a healer. As a Goddess, Morgan LeFay can be less than delicate. She is known for fighting hard, for standing up for her beliefs. She is known for doing left-handed magick. She is skilled in teaching people how to curse and how to use magick to get what they want.

In order to know how to heal, you also have to know how to curse. They are two sides of the same coin. Morgan LeFay is a leader and teacher in this type of magick. She can show you the true path to healing and this doesn't deny the magick that others might deem dangerous. When we know how to heal ourselves, we are better equipped to help heal others. She can lead the way.

Morgan LeFay is the Goddess I have worked with the longest. My experience of her and my interactions with her go deep into my past. I have childhood memories of this Goddess. I knew her before I knew any other deity. She is my first love. And I hold this relationship and what I have learned from her as sacred truth.

HER STORY

The bow of the barge scraped against the sand bottom of the lake. It bobbed up and down slightly, sending ripples across the water. Morgan LeFay sat in the prow of the small boat with the head of her brother resting in her lap. A focused ear could hear the steady dripping sound of Arthur's blood falling on the wooden boards of the boat. Morgan's brother was wounded, dying. There was no chance to bring him back; he would not survive. Morgan knew this, and yet she used her magick to push the boat swiftly across the waters, taking him to Avalon. If there was any chance to save his life, Avalon was the only place where that might be possible.

Morgan was High Priestess of Avalon. She was one of the few that knew the spells and incantations that were required to enter the island hidden by mist and magick. As the boat bobbed along, slowly pushing through the water, she stood, making the gestures and speaking the words needed to leave the world of man and enter the world of magick.

Although she had done this magickal pattern many times, her heart raced, tinged with fear; she could feel the beating of it in her throat. Arthur's enemies pursued them, and if she was not swift in getting him to the isle, they may both be caught. Ultimately, her fear was baseless; she spoke the sacred chant and the mists lowered. The boat was drawn deeper into the Otherworld, away from their enemies, closer to the Goddess.

Arthur stirred, groaning slightly, the blood still dripping from the mortal wound he had received. Without the full magick of Avalon, Morgan would not be able to heal that wound. It had been inflicted using magick, and the only way to stop the flow of blood was with magick.

The boat scraped against the shore as two young priestesses came to the edge of the water. Using magick, the women lifted the wounded king out of the boat and carried him up the hillside and back to the temple. Morgan knew that their enemies would not stop until they knew Arthur was dead. They would find their way to the isle of magick even if it took decades. She had only one choice to save Arthur and to save Avalon.

The priestess of the sacred isle unleashed her magick on the land, creating a cocoon of protection that swirled and roiled out across the island. Her magick poured out from her, separating the world of man from the world of Fae. She put up a barrier, a filter. She exhausted herself as her power flowed out, closing the open spaces between the worlds so anyone seeking them out would be lost. Morgan created a barrier that would hold Arthur in its healing folds until the king could rise again.

MORGAN LEFAY CORRESPONDENCES

+ Lakes

+ Swords

- Herbcraft
- Mist/Fog
- Magick

——◆•◆•◆——•

MORGAN LEFAY RITUAL:
HEART HEALING

——◆•◆•◆——•

This ritual is written for one person to do as a solitary, but it can be easily modified for a group. It involves a trance journey. If doing this ritual with a group, have one of the group members read the trance journey. If you are doing this ritual on your own, record the trance journey and play it back for yourself.

SUPPLIES

rose quartz

sword

image or statue of Morgan LeFay

fresh flowers

incense charcoal

fire-proof container

yarrow

salt scrub

food offering

SET UP

For this ritual you will need a piece of rose quartz, a sword, an image or statue of Morgan LeFay, and a vase of fresh flowers all set up on your altar space. Set up your altar with the image of Morgan

LeFay in front of the vase of flowers. In front of the image, place the rose quartz and then leave the sword laying across the altar with the sword pointing west, if possible.

For the pre-ritual setup you will need incense charcoal, yarrow, a fire-proof bowl, salt scrub, some food, and a glass of water. Take a cleansing bath or shower before starting this ritual. Do a salt scrub while in the water, allowing anything stuck in your spirit body to flow down the drain. When you get out of the bath, allow yourself to air dry.

While drying, light charcoal in a fireproof container on the ground between your legs. Put the yarrow on the charcoal and stand over the smoke. Let the smoke cleanse your spirit and help to shift your energy. Let the smoke begin the call to Avalon and Morgan LeFay.

RITUAL

Put on the clothes that you will wear to ritual and move into your ritual space. Take a deep breath, and as you exhale, make a sound. Repeat this process three times. Pick up the sword, face the west, and cast your circle. Imagine thick mist, thick fog, pushing through the sword, forging a bubble around you.

Turn and face the north; draw an invoking pentacle with your sword, locking in this energy. Continue to turn to the east, see/feel the fog pouring out of the blade of the sword, draw an invoking pentacle locking in the energy. Turn to face the south, draw an invoking pentacle. Turn again, back to the west and draw another invoking pentacle to lock in the corners. Hold the sword, pointing it to the sky, filling the top of your circle with mist, and draw an invoking pentacle. Place the point of the sword on the ground, see the mists filling in the bottom of the circle, and draw an invoking pentacle to lock in the energy.

Face the north, holding the sword across your hands. If it is comfortable for you, get on your knees; if not, stay standing. Raise the sword up like an offering with your palms out and say this:

I call upon Earth. I call upon the land of
Avalon. I call upon the sacred isle of
healing. Welcome to my circle, Earth.

Stand up, lower the sword, and move to the east.

Get on your knees and raise the sword up flat across your palms, facing the east. Say this:

I call upon Air. I call upon the sky of Avalon.
I call upon the sacred words of healing.
Welcome to my circle, Air.

Stand up, lower the sword, and move to the south.

Get on your knees and raise up the sword, facing the south. Say this:

I call upon Fire. I call upon the warmth of
Avalon. I call upon the sacred fires of
healing. Welcome to my circle, Fire.

Stand up, lower the sword, and move to the west.

Get on your knees and raise up the sword, facing the west. Say this:

I call upon Water. I call upon the sea of
Avalon. I call upon the sacred waters of
healing. Welcome to my circle, Water.

Stand up, lower the sword, and move to face your altar.
Say this:

> Great being, Morgan LeFay, I call you into my
> circle. Queen of the Fae. Priestess of Avalon. Magi-
> cian and Witch. You are welcome here. I ask
> for your guidance and wisdom, for your talents
> in the healing arts. I call you here great one.
> Morgan LeFay, be here now!

Pick up the rose quartz and lie down. Place the rose quartz on your heart and start the trance induction.

TRANCE

Open your inner Witch's eye, that third eye that sits right between and above your normal seeing eyes. With this eye open you will find yourself in front of the door that leads to your Place of Power. Hold the intention of seeing Morgan LeFay and knock three times. Turn the handle and walk through the door, ending up in the center of your Place of Power. Scan the edges of your Place of Power until you see a path to Avalon. (Pause…)

When the path becomes clear, take a step onto it and begin to walk forward. Step by step, let your feet carry you closer and closer. As you follow along the path, take note of any plants or animals that may be near you. Breathe in, noticing any scents on the air. Listen to any noises around you.

In the distance you begin to hear the gentle lapping of water against a shoreline. And as you follow a bend in the path, you come to the shoreline. The sand crunches beneath your feet as the soft lapping continues in a rhythmic pattern.

Take a moment to look out over the water. Out on the water you can see a boat moving closer and closer to your spot on the shoreline. The boat is swift, moving quickly across the small bobbing waves. There is a dark figure with a pole pushing the boat through the water, closer and closer to you. The boat scrapes against the shore and the dark figure beckons you to come aboard.

You step onto the boat and the dark figure pushes away from the land. You can feel the weightlessness of the boat floating along the water, gently bobbing up and down as the dark figure continues to push along the bottom of the lake. In the distance the sacred isle of Avalon begins to take shape. The boat continues to move closer and closer and the details of the island become clear.

From the boat you can see groves of apple trees, a temple, and a large wellhead. There is a small deck on the shore and the dark figure pulls the boat right up to the landing dock. You step off of the boat and a voice calls to you from the path ahead. The voice calls your name and the figure speaking steps forward, their shape becoming clear. It is Morgan LeFay.

She reaches out her hand, beckoning you to follow. The two of you walk together in comfortable silence, moving deep into the grove of apple trees. Morgan LeFay reaches out her hand to the ground in front of you and twirls her fingers. From the ground, flowers, branches, and buds grow rapidly and form a soft bed in the comfort of the trees. Morgan LeFay invites you to lie down.

The branches comfortably hold your weight; they are soft and supportive beneath you. Once you are settled, she places her hands on your heart. The scent of apple blossoms fills the air and you can hear the sound of flowing water somewhere in the distance. You feel the warmth, the healing glow, cascading off of her hands and into your heart. The sweet pink glow of fresh apples fills your heart space, releasing any obstacles, clearing any blocks, and bringing healing and health.

As she offers you her healing power she speaks with you and you have time to ask her questions. (Pause) The healing energy continues to grow, expanding from your heart space and filling up your entire body. Morgan LeFay speaks to you again, sharing how to best keep your heart clear. (Pause)

The pressure of her hands on your heart recedes, and as you open your eyes again in the grove of trees, she is gone. You get up from the bed of the forest and it also disappears. Your feet carry you forward, back to the shoreline where the boat waits. The dark figure beckons for you to step onto the boat. Again, you do, and the boat begins to move forward along the water, carrying you back to your Place of Power.

The boat moves swiftly and reaches the opposite shore quickly. You hop onto the sandy shore and follow the path back to the center. Step by step, your feet move along the path that brought you to the shoreline. When you reach the center of your Place of Power, take a breath, step back through the door, and close your inner eye.

Notice the edges of your physical body and pull them in. Breathe into the bottom of your feet and the palms of your hands. Let yourself become fully present in your body, and when you feel ready, open your eyes. Place your hands on the rose quartz and feel the thrum of the newly charged stone, full of the power of Avalon.

Take a moment to absorb this feeling. Place the stone back on the altar. Place some of the food in front of the image of Morgan LeFay and then eat some yourself. Drink some of the water and allow yourself to be present. Speak your gratitude out loud to Morgan LeFay. Tell her of your experience and what you want to hold on to.

When you feel complete, say this:

Great being Morgan LeFay, thank you for joining
me in my circle. Queen of the Fae. Priestess of Ava-
lon. Magician and Witch. Thank you for being here.
Thank you for your guidance and wisdom. From
this circle I bid you hail and farewell.

Pick up the sword and face the west. Say this:

> *Thank you, Water. Thank you waters of healing*
> *and the sea. Hail and farewell, Water.*

Turn and face the south. Say this:

> *Thank you, Fire. Thank you sacred fires*
> *and the warmth. Hail and farewell, Fire.*

Turn and face the east. Say this:

> *Thank you, Air. Thank you words of healing*
> *and the sky. Hail and farewell, Air.*

Turn and face the north. Say this:

> *Thank you, Earth. Thank you isle of healing*
> *and the land of Avalon. Hail and farewell, Earth.*

Using the sword, draw a banishing pentacle below you, releasing the power of the circle you built. Do the same above. Turn to the west and draw the banishing pentacle, releasing the circle. Repeat this process in the south, again in the east, and finally in the north. Say this:

> *The circle is open, yet unbroken. May the peace*
> *of the Goddess go in my heart. Merry meet,*
> *merry part, and merry meet again.*

The work is done! Hail Morgan LeFay!

OTHER GODDS OF MAGICK

Idunna: Norse, Goddess of the apples of immortality

Thoth: Egyptian, Godd of the written word and knowledge

Hecate: Greek, Goddess of the crossroads and Queen of the Witches

Oshun: Afro-Caribbean, Goddess of sensuality, love, and the flowing water

Freya: Norse, Goddess of sex, war, and love

Airmid: Irish, Goddess of herbology and plants

Cerridwen: Welsh, Goddess of transformation

Circe: Greek, Goddess of herbology and spellcraft

Ariadne: Greek, Goddess of weaving, webs, and labyrinths

Enki: Sumerian, Godd of wisdom

Gwydion: Welsh, Godd of learned magick

Obatala: Afro-Caribbean, Godd of wisdom and magick

Diana: Greek, Goddess of the moon and selfhood

5

DEITIES OF
MYSTERY

The Godds of mystery can help open you up to the cycles of the Universe. They are connected to the ebb and flow of life. These deities can show you how to be a part of the unfolding and take your power back. They can show you the way toward understanding your own mystery and how you fit into the world.

The deities of mystery hold power within them and only share their gifts and information for those willing to do the work and put in the time. They possess secrets of the inner workings of things. They know the magick of the ancients.

In this book, the Godds of mystery are ancient deities. These are Godds so old and ancient that we can never fully understand the depth of their power. You will find them in the movement of the stars, the deep flow of the ocean, the cycles of life. They are a part of us, whether we work with them or not.

DIONYSUS

DIONYSUS HISTORY

Dionysus is a Greek God whose origins are a bit murky. He was called "the last of the Olympians," and there is some evidence that he migrated to Greece from another place. He may have come from Crete, the Middle East, Ethiopia, or North Africa. Arguments have been made for each of these places and they all hold water.

There is solid evidence that makes North Africa seem like a strong potential origin for this wild Godd. He is often depicted wearing skins of tigers and leopards, his chariot drawn by panthers—all of these animals were known to come from North Africa. The trade routes of this time reflect a clear path of cultural overlap and travel. Likely this trade route included bringing the wild Godds of Africa into Greece.

For the Greeks, he was the God of wine, ritual ecstasy, and fertility. He comes with an unrestrained desire, a desire for all things—drink, and sex, and love, and dance, all of it. He is also queer. Dionysus floats between the genders, he delights in making love to all, and he revels in celebrating life in all ways possible.

In many of the polytheist ancient cultures of the world, there is a clear shift from a more earth-based system of worship to a patriarchal (sky father) system of worship. In ancient Greece this change of culture came from what many modern folks refer to as the clash of the Titans. The Titans were the "old Godds." They were the forces of nature: big, uncontainable, wild, and raw.

And then along came Zeus. He fought the Titans along with his fellow Olympians and (spoiler alert) they won. The Olympians were ruled by the Sky Father, Zeus. The new Godds changed the landscape and Zeus changed the rules of society. Zeus—the son of a Titan—overthrew their reign. The world focus was shifted from earth to sky. Dionysus is one of Zeus's children *and* a nod to the old Godds of nature, a deity that doesn't exactly fit into the structure of his family.

Those who need to open to the mystery of life may be called to work with Dionysus. This Godd can help you give into your animal self more. A relationship with Dionysus can show you how to revel in your wild nature. If you find yourself needing to let your hair down or have more fun, Dionysus can help you open those doors and celebrate all the beauty of life.

HIS STORY

In the long ago, Dionysus was married to his love, Ariadne. The tale of their meeting is an interesting one, but it is not the story we tell today. During their travels across the world, Ariadne had a terrible accident and died, passing into the realm of Hades, the Underworld.

Dionysus was grief stricken and vowed to do whatever it would take to bring his beloved back to earth. Only a few immortals possessed the ability to go into the Underworld and return to Earth. Dionysus was one of the few that could make the journey, but he didn't know the way. His immortality also gave him the unique ability to restore life. He knew that if he could get to the Underworld and locate Ariadne, he could return her to the land of the living and they could carry out their days together.

Although Dionysus possessed the skills to restore Ariadne's life, the path to the Underworld was filled with dangers. Many of the dead were lost, confused, angry, and dangerous. He would have to make it through the torrent of souls, locate his beloved, and lead the two of them back to the mortal realms. But his first challenge was finding the gates to Hades.

After searching the countryside for someone to help him, Dionysus came to a deep pool on the coast of Argolid, where there was rumored to be an entrance to the Underworld. There he met Prosymnus, a simple shepherd man, who lived near this pool.

Dionysus beseeched Prosymnus to help him get into the Underworld in order to rescue Ariadne from the grip of Hades. Upon seeing the immortal God, Prosymnus was overcome with love. There was nothing in the world that could compare to the beauty of Dionysus, and the shepherd was smitten by his beauty and his power. Prosymnus wanted to help Dionysus, but he also loved him too much to let him go.

Prosymnus offered to help Dionysus get through the entrance to the Underworld, on one condition: upon his return to earth, he would make love to the shepherd. Dionysus felt the pulsing love of this mortal man hit him like a wave, and in return his own desire began to rise. If the circumstances had been different, Dionysus may have stayed with this mortal on the shores of Argolid for many years, but he needed to bring Ariadne back to earth, and so he promised Prosymnus that upon his return they would become lovers.

The shepherd, his heart full, rowed his beloved Dionysus out into the middle of the deep pool and gave him the details on how to enter the Underworld. With a smile and a kiss, Dionysus dove into the depths of the pool and sought out Ariadne. As soon as he crossed over into the land of the Underworld, Dionysus felt Ariadne's presence as if pulled by a magnet. He was drawn to her location and found her more quickly than he could have imagined possible. He pulled his beloved into an embrace, elated to have found her, and swiftly the two made their way to the borders of the Underworld in order to escape.

When a mortal escapes from the Underworld, they are no longer mortal, but they join the ranks of immortals. It is a rare occurrence and a dangerous transformation to make. As Dionysus and Ariadne made their way out of the boundary and back to earth, he realized that he could not leave his beloved alone on earth. The power of her immortality may have been too much for her to handle. So the young God took her to the safety of Mount Olympus where she would be able to rest and recuperate from her ordeal. It was only upon their arrival at Olympus that Dionysus realized how long they had been away from earth.

For you see, time does not work in the Underworld as it does here on earth. Although the two had only been in the Underworld for a few hours, many years had passed while Dionysus was away. He left Ariadne on Olympus and returned to Argolid to seek out Prosymnus and fulfill his promise.

Sadly, Dionysus was years too late. Prosymnus had been dead for decades, his body put to rest in a beautiful tomb near the pool where he had last seen his beloved God. Because he had made a promise that was unfulfilled, Dionysus knew that the shade of Prosymnus would not be at rest until the promise was completed. His heart hurt thinking of the tender man and the love they could have shared. He hated to imagine the shade of Prosymnus struggling with unrest.

Dionysus knew the only way to give peace to his would-be-love was to fulfill their promise to each other. He took a branch from an olive tree and fashioned it into a phallus, taking time and care to create a piece that would honor Prosymnus and bring satisfaction to the promise that had been made during his life. When the phallus was completed, Dionysus affixed it to the tomb of Prosymnus and made love to his shade, fulfilling his oath and releasing the shade to find peace in the Underworld.

DIONYSUS CORRESPONDENCES

- Thyrsus
- Pine cones
- Jaguar
- Wine
- Music
- Dancing
- Grapes

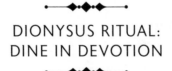

DIONYSUS RITUAL:
DINE IN DEVOTION

I highly recommend performing devotional rituals to Dionysus with a group. Dionysus was followed by a group of wild women called the Maenads. They would work themselves into a frenzy and destroy anything that stood in their way. Although it is possible to work yourself into a frenzy when you are alone, there is something about the power of a group that can bring about true frenzy and abandon. (Please do not go full Maenad, this is not an endorsement of total loss of control.)

The following ritual can be done with a group or solo. It is written as a group ritual and can be easily modified for one person. It can be as mild or wild as you prefer. There is plenty of open space in this ritual for you to increase the frenetic energy. If you are not familiar with this deity, start out slow and let things build. It is a commitment to perform this ritual fully. Performing this ritual is a dedication to developing more ecstasy in your life.

This ritual begins with a dinner. It is best if you can make the meal, but if that's not your thing, ordering food works too. If you cook the meal, stay focused throughout the day while working on the food. Every dish you create should be done holding the intention that this meal is for Dionysus. The preparation process becomes the beginning of the ritual.

Choose music without words to play throughout dinner and afterward. The music should have a primal energy, preferably heavy with drums. Some artists you might consider are James Asher, Dead Can Dance, Nomad, and David Arkenstone. Create a playlist that will last for several hours or at the very least will repeat so you don't have to worry about controlling the music.

SUPPLIES

dinner table setting

tablecloth

fresh flowers

candles

cleansing incense (smudge)

image or statue of Dionysus

wine

wine glass

thyrsus or wand

music playing device

SET UP

Set your table using the "good china." I don't have good china at my house, but I do have some pretty bowls and serving dishes that aren't part of my everyday meals. These are the type of dishes you should pull out for your Dionysus ritual. Use wine glasses and cloth napkins. Set the table with a tablecloth, fresh flowers, and candles. Make it special.

Before your guests arrive, smudge your house. Set up an altar for Dionysus as close to your dining space as possible. On the altar, place an idol or image of Dionysus, a glass of wine, fresh flowers, a candle, a thyrsus (if you don't have a thyrsus, use a wand instead), and whatever else you feel called to add in the moment. Ground and center yourself, allowing yourself to be fully present and ready. Start the music.

RITUAL

As your guests begin to arrive, welcome them and offer them a cleansing smudge. Offer each of the participants a beverage and encourage them to make themselves at home.

Once all participants have arrived, take your thyrsus and cast a circle around your entire ritual space. Start in the north; draw an invoking pentacle in the air creating a boundary of protection. Move to the east, following the same pattern: draw an invoking pentacle and create a boundary. Turn to the south, following the pattern, then to the west, and finally come back to north, completing the circle. Point your thyrsus up and draw a protection pentacle above you. Point your thyrsus down and draw a pentacle of protection below you.

Face the north and say this:

> *I call to the element of Earth. The power of the vine,*
> *the bud, and the leaf, I beckon you into this circle. I*
> *call to the power of growth and regeneration. I*
> *invite the spirit of Earth to join me in this rite.*

Face the east and say this:

> *I call to the element of Air. The power of the song,*
> *the dance, and the music. I beckon you into this*
> *circle. I call to the power of celebration and drum.*
> *I invite the spirit of Air to join me in this rite.*

Face the south and say this:

> *I call to the element of Fire. The power of ecstasy,*
> *the rhythm, the pulse. I beckon you into this circle. I*
> *call to the power of passion and heat. I invite*
> *the spirit of Fire to join me in this rite.*

Face the west and say this:

> *I call to the element of Water. The power of emotion,*
> *the flow, the depth. I beckon you into this circle. I*
> *call to the power of understanding and heart. I*
> *invite the spirit of Water to join me in this rite.*

Face the altar you have built for Dionysus and say this:

> *I call to you, Dionysus. Wild one. Dancer. You*
> *who love with depth and passion. I call to you,*
> *Dionysus. Leader of the Maenads. Reveler in*

divine ecstasy. You are welcome here. I honor you. I
celebrate you. I call to you to join in this ritual
on this night, when we celebrate you Divine
One. Hail and welcome, Dionysus.

Sit and enjoy your meal. During this part of the ritual make sure that everyone has a full glass at all times. Let the wine flow and make toasts to the things that bring you joy in life. (Juice or water can be used in place of wine.) Make toasts to the things that are beautiful in the world. Make toasts to the wildness in your life and call that wildness in. With each toast spoken, offer food or drink to Dionysus. Allow this part of the ritual to be fun, playful, maybe even silly. Toast to the other people you have invited to participate.

As the meal comes to a close, turn up the music or bust out the drums. Continue to pour wine as needed, remembering to include Dionysus as you pour. Allow the music to fuel the revelry. Move your bodies, play drums, and allow the spirit of celebration to move you. Let this continue to rise, growing more frenetic as the evening goes on. Let this ecstasy turn into this chant:

Hey ya, wild God
Come to us, Dionysus
Whose cup of wine brings divine madness
Come to us, Dionysus.

Let the madness build and reach a peak. Allow that energy to come back down, slowly finding stillness and quiet. Sit in the quiet for a moment, give that silence plenty of space and time. Breathe in the energy that you've built and lay it down on the altar to Dionysus.

When you feel ready—after plenty of time has passed—say the following:

Dionysus, wild one, thank you for joining our ritual
this night. Thank you for the song, the dance, the
drink, and the madness. Dionysus, wild one, we
honor you, we thank you, we release you from
this circle. Hail and farewell, Dionysus.

Pick up the thyrsus from the altar and release the pentacle from below and above. Face the north, releasing the circle as you turn to the west. Face the west with your thyrsus and say this:

Thank you element of Water. Thank you
for the emotion, the flow, and the depth.
Hail and farewell, Water.

Turn to the south and say this:

Thank you element of Fire. Thank you for the ec-
stasy, the rhythm, the pulse. Hail and farewell, Fire.

Turn to the east and say this:

Thank you element of Air. Thank you for the song,
the dance, and the music. Hail and farewell, Air.

Finally, face the north and say this:

Thank you element of Earth. Thank you for the
vine, the bud, and the leaf. Hail and farewell, Earth.

Release the circle and say:

The circle is open, but unbroken.

The work is done. Hail Dionysus!

HAPI

HAPI HISTORY

In ancient Egypt, Hapi was more than deity; they were the living Nile River itself. Hapi is a Godd with no gender. They are often described as male, female, both, and neither. Their power came every year in July when the inundation of the Nile happened. The power of Hapi would flood the valley and bring the much-needed water and nutrients that made the Nile a fertile valley instead of a barren desert.

The desert of Egypt and the Nile valley were dry and desolate places for much of the year. The annual flooding of the river was the only thing that made the region livable. It was through the flooding that the land became fertile and food was able to grow. It is no wonder that this power, this elemental shift, was associated with a Godd.

Images from Egyptian dynasties depict Hapi with a pharaoh's beard and a masculine body, but also large breasts and a rounded belly—a balance of what was considered masculine and feminine at the time. They were also seen with blue or green skin, which is the color of the running waters and a symbol of belonging to Otherworld. In reliefs seen from the nineteenth dynasty, Hapi is pictured as two figures, showing the unification of the Upper and Lower Nile regions. Together these two figures hold the two halves of Egypt, keeping things in balance and harmony. In some stories they are called the Father of the Gods, for nothing could exist without them. Hapi was described as caring and balancing.

The annual Nile inundation was referred to as the Arrival of Hapi. Before the waters rushed in, people would leave prayers, blessings, and offerings in the riverbeds for Hapi to touch with their blessing of fertility. These prayers were a calling forth of fertility from the Nile and also a prayer to not overrun the banks and cause damage and flooding.

Hapi can bring more than just the Nile River. This Godd can show us how to find balance in our own bodies, no easy feat for sure! Being in true balance, or what some might call right-size, is not something that can be permanently maintained. We humans are not creatures of balance and it actually takes some work, training, and focus to get in balance. Having a moment of true balance can be a pleasurable experience, especially if it is a feeling that you're not familiar with.

Hapi is an old Godd and one whose worship got a little lost in the annals of time. Their energy is a bit slow, but also very big and potentially dangerous. Imagine a hippopotamus. They seem soft and easy, but they are huge and quick to temper. They move faster than they look and could easily hurt you. That's not to say you need to be afraid of Hapi, but know that this Godd is very ancient, the power of the Nile River itself. Here is Hapi's story as they tell it.

THEIR STORY

All life spills forth from me. I am the beginning of all and I bring life to the land. Before there was anything there was me. I am the Father of the Gods, the Mother of time, and nothing is possible without me. I spend most of my time in my home, the cave beyond the realm of heaven. In my home I gather power, I gather wisdom, I listen, and I watch. From the safety and security of my home in the cave beyond the realm of heaven, I gather power and I grow.

The power, the life force, the energy builds and builds within me. I grow and expand, taking in life and creating power. It causes me to shift and change. As I take on more and more energy, I become too big for my home. The safety of my cave is confining, restrictive, and too small. But then the time comes when I must move on.

The way is not easy. The way is filled with dangers and traps. But the gifts must move and I must share this power with the people, the Gods, and those who are in need. My power must feed the land. This is my gift and sacred duty. The journey takes me first to the heavens. The realm of the heavens is not an area of peace and tranquility. In heaven there are many pitfalls and much false safety. But I grow in power and take on more. I continue to expand. And move on.

Then I move through the Underworld. In the realm of the Underworld there are many dangers. The Underworld is full of tricks, monsters, and confused dead. My energy, my power continues to grow and I attract those that don't know they have died. They are drawn to me like a moth to a flame. This is the moment when my focus, my power is most tenuous. I have to keep my goal in mind. I have to keep collecting the energy of the universe, the flow, but I must not release it to these desperate creatures, no matter how much I feel called to help them.

As I reach the end of the Underworld, I find the opening of the sacred cave in the mountainside. Here the power within me becomes unbearable. The energy crests within me. A full balloon being pushed to the very edges of what it can hold. It is painful and blissful and all-encompassing. I reach the edge of ecstasy, lost between the desire to feel this power flow through me and the need to end the pain of it.

At the mouth of the cave the power, the energy, the pulse crescendos. I burst forth. The power unleashed, released. The undulating intensity pulsates through me. It is beautiful and terrible. The flow of the Nile rushes through my being, filling me with fertility. I am power. I am life. I am the Nile.

Me—the water—rushes down the mountain. An outpouring and flow. The green, fertile water that brings forth all life. It spreads out through the valley. It takes over the dry and dusty areas, soaking them in my juice—my life force. What was barren is filled with life, is filled with me. I wet the offerings left in the dry riverbeds with my kiss and caress. I soak the blessings in my fluids. I bring life to the land.

HAPI CORRESPONDENCES

- Flowing water
- Fertility
- Red barley
- Rivers

HAPI RITUAL: BALANCE, FULLNESS, DELIGHT

This ritual is best performed outdoors near a body of water with space for a few small altar items next to you. As always, with rituals outside, make sure that you are safe and can be relatively undisturbed. I find rituals outdoors best done with other people, for safety reasons, but this ritual is written as a solo endeavor. Modify as needed.

SUPPLIES

blanket

image or statue of Hapi

bowl

biodegradable offering

SET UP

You will need a bowl, a blanket to lie down on or a chair to sit comfortably in, an image or statue of Hapi, and an offering to Hapi (this should be something biodegradable that you can safely put into the running water).

RITUAL

Settle at a place near a body of water where you will be as undisturbed as possible. Lay out your blanket with the bowl, the offering, and image of Hapi on the blanket.

Take a moment to breathe in the air around you. Allow this simple breathing to bring you to a place of clarity and centeredness. Bring yourself into full presence. Using the first two fingers of your dominant hand, cast a circle of desert heat around you. Imagine as you move from quarter to quarter that you are enveloped in the heat of a desert mirage. As you send this energy around your space, see yourself covered by the heat waves of the desert. Remember to close your circle by casting above you and below you.

Turn to face the east and say:

> I call to the powers of Air. I welcome in breath, music, sound, and dawn. I invite the Spirit of Air into my circle to aid in my work. Hail and welcome, Air.

Turn to face the south and say:

> I call to the powers of Fire. I welcome passion, inspiration, energy, and heat. I invite the Spirit of Fire into my circle to aid in my work. Hail and welcome, Fire.

Turn to face the west and say:

> I call to the power of Water. I welcome intuition, flow, grace, and moisture. I invite the Spirit of Water into my circle to aid in my work. Hail and welcome, Water.

Turn to face the north and say:

> I call to the power of Earth. I welcome strength, power, stability, and bone. I invite the Spirit of Earth into my circle to aid in my work. Hail and welcome, Earth.

Pick up your bowl and fill it with the wild water of the place where you are located. Raise the bowl above your head and say:

Hail Hapi. Hail Nile. I call to you Hapi, Godd of
Egypt. I call to your power of inundation. I call to
you, first of the Godds. You are welcome in my circle.
I ask for your gifts of balance, awareness, and grace.
Hail and welcome, Hapi.

Set the bowl of water on your small altar, use that water to anoint yourself on your third eye, and lay down on the blanket.

Allow yourself to relax. Turn your hearing toward the flow of water and let your spirit connect to that flow. Let your edges, your boundaries, open and widen more and more, as if you are becoming droplets of water, but also remember who you are and where you are; listen to the water as it flows. And breathe, breathe deep.

As you breathe, feel the pulse of watery movement through your veins. As you inhale, feel the intake, the expansion, the coming in. As you exhale, feel the release, the contraction, the letting go. Follow this breath, this in and out, letting that power and that energy build within you.

Let this process go on for as long as you feel called to do it. Let the power build. Let yourself be like a battery accepting the charge and the building of the flow. As you breathe, listen to the water. Continue to let that sound fuel your breath and build up the power in your body.

When you feel full, spread your arms and legs and let the flow of water and the flow of your breath find the balance within your skin. Notice where you feel more empty or full and focus bringing your body into balance. Let the energy you have built up within you move to your extremities, your gut, the top of your head, and all throughout your body. Let that energy bring you into balance.

This may take some time. You might discover you come into balance only to immediately lose that balance. This is okay. Keep going, keep shifting the energy, keep working on coming into balance and holding it there for as long as possible. When you feel complete, slowly open your eyes. Hold the balance for as long as you can. Slowly and gently let your breathing return to normal. Let your energy dissipate, releasing the excess back into the earth below you and the running water nearby. Let yourself return to your normal state of being.

Slowly and carefully sit up and gather your offering to Hapi. Move down to the edge of the water and speak from your heart to Hapi. Show your gratitude for the flow of water in the world, in your body, and in your life. Give the offering to Hapi by placing it in the water. Take as much time as you feel called to commune with Hapi in this place of flowing water.

When you feel ready, return to your blanket. Breathe and center yourself. Pick up the bowl of water and raise it above your head. Say this:

> *Hapi, living flow of the Nile. Great Godd of balance,*
> *flow, fertility, and power. Thank you for being pres-*
> *ent in my rite. Thank you for your force and flow.*

Pour the water back on the ground and say:

> *I release you from this circle. I honor you.*
> *I thank you. Hail and farewell, Hapi.*

Turn to the north and say:

> *Thank you, powers of Earth. Thank you strength,*
> *power, stability, and bone. I release you from*
> *this circle. Hail and farewell, Earth.*

Turn to the west and say:

> *Thank you, powers of Water. Thank you intuition,*
> *flow, grace, and moisture. I release you from*
> *this circle. Hail and farewell, Water.*

Turn to the south and say:

> *Thank you, power of Fire. Thank you passion,*
> *inspiration, energy, and heat. I release you*
> *from this circle. Hail and farewell, Fire.*

Turn to the east and say:

> *Thank you, power of Air. Thank you breath,*
> *music, sound, and dawn. I release you*
> *from this circle. Hail and farewell, Air.*

Open the circle of desert heat that you built, sending that energy back to the sands of Egypt. Clap your hands to further dissipate that energy.

The work is done. Hail Hapi!

MITHRAS

MITHRAS CULTURE

I've heard it said that had it not been for Constantine, the Western world would have ended up worshippers of Mithras. It is true that the stories of Mithras and Jesus have much in common, and for a time the two religions functioned side by side, but history shows that the Mithrasian religion was comfortable with other forms of worship and other Godds, while the Christian religion was not.

Both Jesus and Mithras were both of supernatural or "virgin" births. Both were honored as having their birthdays on December 25. Both had wise men attend their births. Both were shepherds with twelve disciples. Both sacrificed their lives and were resurrected. Perhaps these two have the same origins. We may never know.

There is very little known of Mithras and how he was worshipped, which is endlessly fascinating because we actually have quite a bit of information on his temples and priest system. However, the Mithras cult was a secret society and the rituals and rites were likely oral tradition only. Even with all of the temples, iconography, symbology, and priest rankings we know very little about how this cult actually worked.

What we do know is theory at best. It is likely that the practitioners of Mithraism were men only. Honor and worship of Mithras was well known and practiced by Roman soldiers. It is likely that the rituals for Mithras involved some sort of sacred meal. Mithrasian temples had long benches, almost like church pews, in them. These would have been laid upon by the members of the temple when it was time to take a meal together. It was not uncommon in Rome and Greece for the higher classes of society to eat while lying down or lounging.

However, if this cult was so popular amongst the warriors of the time, it is likely that there were other rituals that served these people. No doubt lounging with other warriors, eating a meal, and sharing your God's stories in temple was a fine afternoon well spent. But it seems very unlikely that these type of rituals were the sum total of a warrior God's worship. It leaves us wondering what the common soldier did in their worship of Mithras.

The rituals that may have taken place outside of the temple walls, the initiations, the elevations, the secret runnings of the cult, are pieces of Mithrasian worship that we may never know. The Mithras cults are unique in how much imagery and temple grounds are left behind, yet there is virtually nothing left on why and how these temples were used.

We do know that members of the cult had to be initiated and there were seven ranks to rise up through. It is believed by some Mithraic scholars that the levels of initiation are connected to the seven planets. The members were "united by the handshake," called *syndexioi* in Latin. Most of the temple structures were underground with very little natural light; often a very specifically placed sky light was the only natural light source.

It seems clear to me that much of this cult was connected to the heavens and the constellations, not to mention astrology. Just by looking at the iconography in the images of Mithras—scorpion, bull, twins, sun, moon, dog, snake, lion, chalice—you can see many connections to astronomy and astrology.

There are rumors of modern Mithraic cults that have picked up and are working to reconstruct the practices of the ancient followers, but I've yet to uncover any solidly practicing groups. Any reconstruction would be very loosely based on what we actually know. All of the ritual and worship is totally lost to the hands of time.

HIS STORY

It was time for the hunt. For months the sacred bull had been prepped. He was thick and muscled and powerful, with a white coat of soft fur. He had been fed the sweetest herbs, the best fruits, the finest grains. He was bathed in clear water every day. Every day the priestesses sang the sacred chants, imbuing the bull with the power of the Gods.

The warrior Mithras readied himself as the priestesses readied the bull. For months he trained. For the weeks leading up to the holy day he ate only the prepared foods from the priestesses. He visited the temples of Sol and Oceanus, leaving offerings and gifts as a prayer for their blessing his success.

Although born divine, the old ones required Mithras to earn his place among them. As the warrior of the Gods he had to prove himself over and over again. The challenge with the bull was only the latest in a long line of challenges from the Titans. Forever they were asking him to prove his worth. Forever they were forcing him to step up and show his mettle.

The day of the challenge the bull was dressed with the *dorsuale*, the sacred cloth that was embroidered with the images of the sun, the stars, and the moon. He was given the final draught that would take over his body, fueling his rage and power. As the drink took hold, the bull was released in the temple square. The bull's nostrils began to flair, his blood began to boil, and he cried out in his rage.

The priests and priestesses of the temple retreated to safety, waiting for the champion of the Gods to appear.

As the bull was prepared, so was Mithras. The priestesses washed him in a bath of the sacred herbs. They oiled his skin and spoke the words of blessings as they dressed him. He was dressed in simple breeches with a knee-length tunic of blue fabric covering his muscled arms. On top of the tunic they put a cloak of red around his neck. A knife was strapped to his leg, the hilt of it peeking out from inside of his boot, with a sword placed around his waist. Finally as the priestess spoke the final words of power to the Gods' warrior, they put the phrygian cap upon his head. This was the soft conical hat with the tip folded to the front, which represented liberty.

Once the cap was on the head of the warrior, his eyes shifted, glowing with the God-power that came from deep within him. His God-self gleamed out from his dark eyes, clear and visible to anyone that should look upon him. Immediately, his head cocked to the side as he felt the call of the bull.

There was no hurry, there was no rush. Mithras knew what Sol and Oceanus expected of him. He knew the challenge he must complete. This wasn't just a game the old Gods wanted to play (although that was part of it), it was a rite for the people. Killing the bull, taking the life of the powerful creature was a blessing to the warriors of Rome. To the soldiers that put their lives on the line for the Republic. He completed these tasks set before him to honor those that honored him, to feed them, to give them power.

Mithras stalked through the temple grounds, sword in hand. He knew exactly where the bull was and he knew the bull felt him coming. The two warrior forces came together as a blessing. As Mithras entered the center temple grounds the bull stood waiting, nostrils flaring and muscles tense. There would be no battle; Mithras must win his right to kill the bull by sheer power alone. Both had received the sacred blessings, both had received the sacred food, both had been prepared for this meeting of power.

The warrior bowed to his prey, holding the sword outstretched on his palms as a display of the act to come. The bull shook his massive head and pawed the ground several times before snorting at the God.

Mithras's eyes shone with his God power. He held the sword and pointed to the bull with its tip. The intensity of his force, of his being, shot through the blade. The bull took a staggering step backward, hit by the power. There the two stood facing each other, breathing deeply.

Time stood still. The God waited, knowing his will was the force that would win. Mithras continued to hold his ground, sending out his willpower to the beast. Finally, finally, the bull imperceptibly nodded his head. He turned away from the warrior and sat on the ground. As the force of his body landed on the earth, the ground shook, but Mithras stood solid and unwavering.

He strode forward, confident and calm, the sword out in front of him. Mithras leapt onto the back of the bull. With his left knee on the bull and his right foot pinning the rear of the animal to the ground, the warrior pulled back the mighty head by placing his fingers in the nose of the beast. The wind on the temple grounds picked up and his red cape billowed out behind him. The muscles of the bull were taught but yielding as Mithras plunged the blade into the neck of the creature below him.

The world shifted. The temple grounds elongated and pressed closer together. Mithras and bull were frozen in place. Creatures came. A dog jumped up, reaching for the wound and the blood seeping from it. A serpent slithered its way under the beast, lunging with its narrow head for the blood-soaked tear in the bull's neck. A scorpion scuttled out, grabbing the genitals of the bull in its pinchers.

The temple grounds continued to shift and change, pulling and pushing, pressing down on the God and the bull beneath his legs. Drops of the bull's blood fell to the ground and wheat sheaves sprang up from those blessed places. A raven landed near the tail of the bull, croaking out sounds that almost sounded like the blessings from the priestesses.

At the same time, in the sky above them Sol appeared to the right and his sister Selene appeared to the left. The sun and the moon both shone their life force and light brightly on the scene. The warp and weft of time folded over, shaking up the gathering and reverberating out across the land. The blessing of Mithras was granted to every Roman legionnaire, whether they paid him homage or not. An extra heartbeat was granted to every officer. The power pulsated throughout Rome as the blood of the bull continued to drip onto the temple grounds and the scene stood frozen.

Time went by; whether it was a second or a century no one could say. But the challenge of Sol and Oceanus was complete. Mithras slew the bull. His blessing spilt forth, forward, and beyond. Again the challenge of the Titans to Mithras was completed and Rome was blessed for it.

MITHRAS CORRESPONDENCES

- Astrology
- Sun signs
- Sun
- Moon
- Bull
- Dog
- Wheat
- Snake

◆•◆•◆

MITHRAS RITUAL: WARRIOR POWER

◆•◆•◆

Warriors are not just soldiers and those trained for battle. Warriors are those who face hardship and keep going. Warriors are those who fall down and get back up again. Warriors are those who stand up for others and do what is right. Warriors come in all shapes, sizes, and gender expressions. And in these modern times of change and expansion, I believe that Mithras is willing and able to meet us all at whatever level of warrior we are ready to express.

The following ritual will help you connect to the energy of Mithras as a God of the warriors. This can help you to prepare to get into a challenging situation, strengthen your reserves if you're already in a challenging situation, or even level up your warrior hit points (so to speak). This ritual is intended for all people who want to tap into the power of Mithras.

This ritual is written for a solitary practitioner but can easily be modified for a coven or group.

SUPPLIES

charm or talisman

red altar cloth

two blue candles

athame

image or statue of Mithras

frankincense incense

fireproof container

feather or fan

bowl of salt water

drum

SET UP

For this ritual you will need an item that can be charged and that is safe to carry with you. It could be a small dagger or knife, it could be a charm or talisman, it could be a stone or crystal. You will need to determine the best object for you to use in this charging.

On the altar, place a red altar cloth, two blue candles, and your athame. Also place an image or statue of Mithras, frankincense incense and fireproof container, a feather or fan, a bowl of salt water, a drum, and the item that you will charge.

RITUAL

Set up your altar and allow yourself to come into a place of feeling grounded and centered. Release anything that you don't need into the earth below you and breathe deeply. Feel your center and pull in all of your parts and pieces. Reel in anything that isn't fully present and in your body.

When you feel fully present, pick up the bowl of water and face the north. Sprinkle the salt water around your circle, moving in a clockwise direction. As you move through your space, say this:

I use this salt and this water to cleanse my space.

Set down the bowl of water and pick up the incense.

Light the incense and face the north. Blow the incense around your space using the fan or feather. Walk in a clockwise circle, allowing the incense to help you clear your magickal space. Say this:

I use this smoke to charge my circle.

Set down the incense and pick up your athame.

Hold up your athame, pointing it north and draw an invoking pentacle. As you draw the pentacle, visualize it filled with moonlight. Continue to cast your circle, turning to the east with your athame pointed in that direction. Visualize this pentacle filled with sunlight. With your athame, continue to create your circle by turning to the south. Draw an invoking pentacle and visualize it filled with sunlight. Continue drawing your circle, turning to the west. Here fill the pentacle with moonlight. Finally, come back to the north, completing the circle by drawing a pentacle above you with sunlight and a pentacle below you with moonlight.

Once your circle casting is complete, say this:

*I call upon the powers of the elements to join in my
circle. I call to the north, east, south, and west. I call
to the center, to the above and the below. I invite in
the powers to aid me in work that will build
my warrior spirit and hone my craft.*

Stand with your legs open and your arms crossed over your
chest. Stomp your foot at a slow, steady rhythm, like a heartbeat.
Chant his name slowly, allowing the syllables to elongate and
stretch out as they roll over your tongue. *MIIIIITH-RAAAAS.*
Repeat this three times, speaking as slowly and deeply as possible.
Say this:

*Mithras, warrior, virgin born
To you whom all the soldiers were sworn
Strong and solid, wise and bold,
I call you now into the fold
Come into my circle, cast times three
Bring forth your power, share it with me*

Light the candles on your altar and pick up the object for
charging. Take a moment to speak from your heart, calling on the
warrior energy of Mithras. Share with him why you need to increase your warrior energy. Ask him for his guidance and power to
help you step up. Speak your truth and feel his presence.

Chant his name again. Continue to chant, letting the power
build up. Allow your voice to be as deep as possible, elongating the
vowels and building the energy of his power. When you feel ready,
which may take more time than feels comfortable, make a single
tone and allow all of that energy and power you have built up to
flow into your object. Feel the energy move through your body,

through your hands, and into the talisman. Allow the power of Mithras to imbue the object with a warrior's power.

Sit in this space for a moment. Just be. Breathe and ground. Let any excess energy rain down around you or sink back into the earth. When you feel ready, place the object back on the altar and take a moment to speak your gratitude out loud to Mithras.

Say this:

> *Mithras, warrior, virgin born*
> *To you whom all the soldiers were sworn*
> *My gratitude I offer to thee*
> *And release you from my circle, cast times three*
> *Hail and farewell, Mithras.*

Stand up and bow to the altar. Say this:

> *I thank the below and the above. I thank the center.*
> *I thank the powers of the elements for joining my*
> *circle. I thank the west, south, east, and north. I*
> *offer my gratitude to the powers that aided me in*
> *my work to build my warrior spirit and hone*
> *my craft. Hail and farewell, elements.*

Pick up your athame, pointing it below, and draw a banishing pentacle. Repeat this with your athame pointing above. Then turn toward the north, releasing the circle that you created. Turn to the west and draw a banishing pentacle, releasing the moonlight. Turn to the south and draw a banishing pentacle, releasing the sunlight. Turn to the east and draw a banishing pentacle, releasing the sunlight. Finally, turn to the north and draw a banishing pentacle, releasing the moonlight. The work is done! Hail Mithras!

OTHER GODDS OF MYSTERY

Isis: Egyptian, Goddess of motherhood, healing, and mystery

Ereskigal: Sumerian, Goddess of the underworld

Odin: Norse, Godd of mystery, galdr, and the written word

Epona: Gaulish, Goddess of horses and fertility

Taranis: Celtic, Godd of thunder

Arianrhod: Welsh, Goddess of the night sky

Maat: Egyptian, Goddess of balance

Maya: Hindu, Goddess of illusion

Nornir: Norse, three Goddesses of past, present, and wyrd

Persephone: Greek, Goddess of the underworld

Despoina: Greek, Goddess of fertility and the mysteries

Dionn: Roman, Goddess of love

Aion: Greek, Godd of the ages and the wheel of time

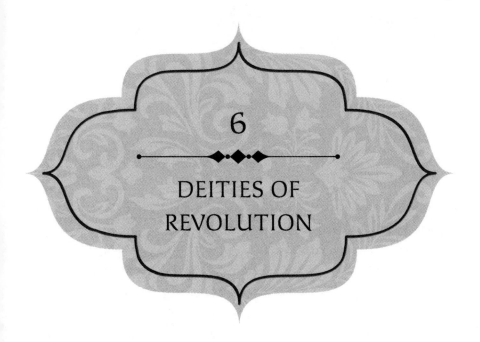

6

DEITIES OF REVOLUTION

The Godds of revolution show us the way to make radical transformation in our lives and in the larger world around us. These are the Godds that were radical in their own time. These are the Godds that shook things up and can still reveal to us how to step into revolution. This is more than personal work; this is work for changing the world.

We are always facing revolution of some shape or form. We go through personal revolutions when we gather information, learn new skills, or open to new relationships. We go through collective revolutions when we change our patterns of inclusivity, language, and understanding in our groups and tribes. We go through revolutions of society when we stand up, fight oppression, and care for the earth. Life is full of revolutions.

The Godds of revolution included in this book were known to be revolutionary in their own time. These are the deities of and for the people. The Godds included in this section are the Godds that can teach us how to stand up and fight for our lives and what we believe in.

ARADIA

ARADIA CULTURE

She is a much-misunderstood Goddess, Aradia. Early in my days of teaching on Godds, I felt that there was nothing more important than knowing the origins of a deity, and therefore their truth. I felt that knowing the origins of a Godd meant that you knew the strongest most potent force of that entity. Although I still believe it is important to know the origins of a Godd, I no longer hold the belief that "older is better." Learning about Aradia is one of the reasons my feelings changed.

Aradia is an Italian Goddess, born of Diana and Lucifer. In 1899, Charles Leland, an American writer and folklorist, published a book called *The Gospel of Aradia*, which was supposedly given to him by an Italian Witch named Maddalena. Charles Leland wrote several books about Italian Witchcraft and some even believe that he was initiated into an Italian coven. There isn't any older mention of a Goddess named Aradia in any written story, name, or other folk tale, but that doesn't mean she wasn't known earlier than 1899. We just don't have record of it.

Although no clear nor solid evidence has been found, there is more to dissect here than just whether Maddalena existed or if Aradia was invented in 1899. The book Leland published didn't just come from the information he received from Maddalena. Leland was quite open about taking many spells from other Italian sources.

In fact, the book Charles Leland wrote is a rather interesting spell book, but very little of it is about Aradia. Mostly it is a devotional to Diana. Which begs the question: who is Aradia?

It's true that her history and origins are sketchy. However, the power that she brings to the people is what is important. Aradia was sent to earth at a time of great need. She was sent to earth to teach the people Witchcraft, to help the people take back their power. Aradia helped people fight against oppression. Diana charged her only daughter to show people the power of Witchcraft.

The more that we call on her, the stronger she gets. The Godds evolve just like humans do. We can't know the details of her origins, but we do know who she has become. Aradia has been a part of the modern Witchcraft movement since its inception. And over the last few years she has started to show up for many Witches and Pagans.

Many popular writers and leaders in the modern Pagan tradition have started to tell her stories, invoke her in rituals, and connect to her again. A hashtag (#weareAradia) was created to offer magickal support to those fighting oppression. All of this comes at a time when our political and social climate is calling for the Witches to step up and fight back. It is no wonder that Aradia is awakening and being called upon by more and more Witches across the globe.

HER STORY

Aradia sat in the window of her room at the temple of Diana, the realm of her mother, the Great Goddess. It was dusk, the pink and orange hues of day being swallowed by the dark purple of night. It was the sweet between time, being neither day nor night, but a moment when both things are possible. The air was warm, with a slight breeze sending a ripple of gooseflesh up her young arms. This was her favorite place in all of Diana's temples. Here Aradia could see to the ocean, to the deepest reaches of space, to the human realms below. From here the view was magick.

A shift in the air, an inhale and release, blasted through the room. Aradia recognized this as the appearance of Diana on the temple grounds. She rose from her window, excited to see her mother. The temple crackled with magick when Diana was home. Aradia ran through the bedroom door, following the marbled passageway to the waiting rooms on the floor below.

When she reached the waiting room, Aradia stopped in her tracks. There was something terribly wrong and it was written all over Diana's face. "Mother, what is it?" Aradia whispered, afraid to come too close. Diana was a benevolent Goddess, but she was not to be fussed with when in a state.

"Come, my daughter," Diana said stretching out a hand to her Aradia. "Come, we have much to discuss."

Aradia grasped the outstretched hand and Diana offered a comforting squeeze. They moved together to a lounge chair and both sat down, close enough that their legs touched. "Much is wrong in the human realm, my daughter. Much that I was hoping would find resolution is only getting worse."

Diana lifted her other hand, laying her palm flat, and an image appeared to float above it. Scene after scene of human suffering, starvation, and forced servitude flashed in and out on Diana's hand. Each snapshot worse than the last—sadness, famine, war, struggle, death, and powerlessness. It was terrible. Diana closed her hand and the image dissipated.

"Is it time?" Aradia asked bravely, squaring her shoulders.

For decades Diana had been training her daughter in the arts of Witchcraft. Painstakingly, day after day, Aradia studied the herbs, potions, incantations, and spells that were the art of the wise. This was a special magick that Diana alone, of all the Gods, possessed. It was a skill and a talent that she shared only with her daughter.

Diana was always clear that the gift of Witchcraft belonged to Aradia, but it was not a gift she could keep to herself. Since the time she was born, Aradia knew that at some point she would go to the human realm and share the skills and magick that Diana had given her with the people of Earth. Aradia knew by the vision her mother had shown her that the time had come.

"Yes, my daughter," Diana responded, a stoic look transforming her face. As soon as the sentence was finished half dozen priestesses entered the room and the preparations began.

CORRESPONDENCES FOR ARADIA

* Rue

* Vervain

* Lemons

* Moon

"LIBERATION SONG" BY SUZANNE STERLING

Our voices will rise in liberation song

Our voices will rise in liberation song

When we are singing, we are Aradia

When we are dancing, we are Aradia

When we all rise up, we are Aradia

We are the Witches, we are Aradia

ARADIA RITUAL: LEMON BLESSINGS

One of the spells in the *Gospel of Aradia* is the lemon spell. This is done as a blessing for protection. I have worked with Aradia for several years and have used a modification of this spell many times. I share this modified spell working with you now.

I love this spell/ritual because it does have older origins. It could be an ancient Italian spell or it could have been written in the late 1800s. It doesn't really matter how old it is; it is a spell that has been worked with success for at least two hundred years. Not too shabby.

This ritual is written for a solitary practitioner, but could be easily modified for a group or coven. For a group, have all participants prepare with a ritual bath before coming to the ritual space.

SUPPLIES

lemons

stick pins with colored heads

red ribbon

fresh flowers

a libation cup

wine

an image or statue of Aradia

crescent moon symbol

two silver candles

frankincense

bowl of salt

bowl of water

athame

wand

bell

candle for lighting a room

SET UP

For this working you will need a lemon, stick pins with colored heads, and a red ribbon near or next to your altar. On the altar place a vase of fresh flowers, a cup and a bottle of wine, an image or statue of Aradia, a symbol of the crescent moon, two silver candles, frankincense, a bowl of salt, a bowl of water, your athame, your wand, and a bell. If possible, keep all electronic lights turned off and have the room lit with candles or a fire only.

RITUAL

Take a cleansing bath and ritually prepare for the working. Anoint yourself with your favorite oil and go into the ritual space skyclad. If skyclad isn't comfortable for you, put on freshly cleaned, simple, loose clothes.

Light the candles (not the silver candles) or fire in your ritual space. Ground and center yourself, bringing your energy and spirit fully present. Pick up the bell and ring it as you walk around your ritual space. Focus on clearing energy as you move through the room.

Set down the bell and pick up your athame. Use your athame to scoop three measures of salt into the cup of water. Draw a pentacle in the water with your athame three times, charging the water. Set down your athame, then take the bowl of salt water and sprinkle this around your circle, focusing on cleansing your space.

Set down the bowl of salt water and pick up your frankincense. Light the incense and then walk it around the circle of your space. Use this smoke to charge your ritual space.

Set down the incense, but keep it burning as the ritual goes on. Light the silver candles on the altar and then pick up your wand. Move to the north and begin to cast your circle. Start in the north, moving to the east, the south, the west, and again to the north. Point your wand outward, creating a solid barrier between your ritual space and the outside world. Move into the center of your space and close your circle by directing your energy above you and below you, creating a sphere of protection around your space.

Set down your wand and pick up your athame. Move to the east, point your athame in this direction, draw an invoking pentacle, and say:

> Hail to the guardians of the east. I call upon the
> dawn, the wind, music and sound. I call Air into my
> circle to aid in my work. Hail and welcome, Air.

Move to the south, point your athame in this direction. Draw an invoking pentacle and say:

> Hail to the guardians of the south. I call upon the
> day, the heat, the spark and flame. I call Fire into
> my circle to aid in my work. Hail and welcome, Fire.

Move to the west and point your athame in this direction. Draw an invoking pentacle and say:

> *Hail to the guardians of the west. I call*
> *upon the dusk, the flow, the drip and the*
> *depth. I call Water into my circle to aid in*
> *my work. Hail and welcome, Water.*

Move to the north and point your athame in this direction. Draw an invoking pentacle and say:

> *Hail to the guardians of the north. I call*
> *upon the night, the soil, the bone and the*
> *ground. I call Earth into my circle to aid*
> *in my work. Hail and welcome, Earth.*

Move into the center of your circle, point your athame to the center point. Draw an invoking pentacle and say:

> *Hail to the guardians of Ether. I call upon*
> *the unknown, the everything, the betwixt and*
> *between. I call Ether into my circle to aid*
> *in my work. Hail and welcome, Ether.*

Place your athame back on the altar and raise your hands above you in the Goddess pose. Say this:

> *Aradia, Queen of the Witches. Aradia, daughter of*
> *the moon and the light bringer. Aradia, first Witch,*
> *revolutionary, edge walker. I call to you, great one. I*
> *call you into my circle to guide my work. I ask for your*
> *spirit to aid my personal revolution. Aradia, I honor*
> *you. Aradia, be here now. Hail and welcome, Aradia.*

Pour a glass of wine into the cup as an offering to Aradia.

Sit in quiet meditation. Allow yourself to focus on the blessings that you have in your life. Take some time in your meditation to count these blessings, seeing clearly your gifts in life. Allow yourself to feel full of these blessings. When you can feel your cup of blessings overflowing, allow yourself to shift your focus to the blessings that you want to call in.

If working with a group, give time for each person to share their blessings. If working alone, name your blessings out loud. Pick the lemon up off the altar. When complete, take the pins and name the blessings that you want to call in, one at a time, pushing a pin into the lemon as you name each one. If working in a group, take turns naming what you are calling in. If working alone, name what you call in out loud.

Take the red ribbon and wrap it around the lemon. As you do this, feel the energy being held in place, creating a type of blessing magnet, helping to draw what you really want toward you. As you wrap the ribbon, repeat the following chant:

Aradia, Aradia, I implore thee
Bring forth these blessings
Let them be drawn to me
By magick and spell
By blood and by bone
This working is done
Bring these blessings home

When finished, place the lemon back on the altar close to the image of Aradia. Take a moment to speak your heartfelt gratitude to Aradia for manifesting your desires, as if you already have them.

Stand facing the altar in Goddess pose and say this:

Thank you Aradia, Queen of the Witches. Thank
you, Aradia, daughter of the moon and the light
bringer. Thank you Aradia, first Witch, revolution-
ary, edge walker. I am grateful to you, Goddess.
Thank you for guiding my work. Thank you for
your aiding my personal revolution. I release you
from this circle. Hail and farewell, Aradia.

Snuff out the silver candles.

Pick up your athame and hold it pointing to the center of your ritual space, draw a banishing pentacle. Say this:

Hail to the Guardians of Ether. I release
the unknown, the everything, the betwixt
and between. I thank you, Ether, for aiding
in my work. Hail and farewell, Ether.

Point your athame to the north, draw a banishing pentacle, and say:

Hail to the guardians of the north. I release
the night, the soil, the bone, and the ground.
I thank you, Earth, for aiding in my
work. Hail and farewell, Earth.

Turn to the west, pointing your athame. Draw a banishing pentacle and say:

Hail to the guardians of the west. I release the dusk,
the flow, the drip, and the depth. I thank you, Wa-
ter, for aiding in my work. Hail and farewell, Water.

Continue turning, facing the south. Point your athame in this direction and draw a banishing pentacle. Say this:

Hail to the guardians of the south. I release the day,
the heat, the spark, and flame. I thank you, Fire, for
aiding in my work. Hail and farewell, Fire.

Turn again to the east, point your athame, and draw a banishing pentacle. Say this:

Hail to the guardians of the east. I release the dawn,
the wind, music, and sound. I thank you, Air, for
aiding in my work. Hail and farewell, Air.

Set down your athame and pick up your wand. Start by pointing your wand below you and then above you, releasing the energy that you built up. Then face the north and turn widdershins, pulling down the circle that you built up. As the energy is released, snap your fingers and clap your hands, clearing away the rest of it. Say this:

The circle is open, yet unbroken. May the power of
Araida go in my heart. Merry meet. Merry part.
And merry meet again. Blessed be!

The work is done! Hail Aradia!

THOR

THOR CULTURE

Thor is described as being a massive hulk of a man with a large red beard, red hair, and occasionally red eyes as well. His appetite was well known and seemed to be endless. Some descriptions of him paint him as rather dull and witless—all brawn and no brain—but he was excellent with battle tactics. He was not known for his sense of humor anciently, but my modern experience of him suggests that he may have grown over the years.

Although Thor was a prominent God throughout the Germanic and Scandinavian regions, most of the written texts we have of him are from Iceland. This is true for much of what we know of the Norse and Germanic deities.

One of the messages that's repeated over and over about the Thunder God is that he was a God of the people. The people who gave him offerings were warriors, farmers, mothers, clan leaders, and healers. Thor was the "everyman's" God and protector of all the realms.

His greatest enemy is the sea serpent Jormungand, a monster capable of destroying all the worlds. Jormungand has a serpent-like body that is wrapped around Midgard, the human realms. The sea snake keeps this realm hostage, ever tightening his grip on the land. This is further evidence of Thor being a God of humanity, as his greatest enemy is the beast working to destroy the human realms.

However, Jormungand is not Thor's only enemy. He also fights against the giants, the Jotnar. The Jotnar are the forces of nature, the big primeval forces that cannot be contained. Thor's work is never done, and in the sagas (a collection of tales from the Scandinavian ancients), he never finishes fighting the Jotnar. These forces will always exist, they will always be present, but he helps to keep them under control.

Thor was also called upon by the people to "hallow" places, items, or events. There are runic inscriptions and prayers to Thor that survive today in which people asked Thor to hallow their harvest, their wedding, or some other human event. *Hallow* means to honor as holy. Clearly, Thor was more than just a protector; he was also one who offered blessings.

His weapon of choice, his hammer, called Mjölnir, was able to destroy, crush, and obliterate. A basic concept of magick—what can cure can kill—suggests that Thor's hammer was also able to grow, bless, and mend. Thor was known as the thunder, while Mjölnir was the lightning.

The relationship of thunder and lightning as symbols of health and fertility can be seen in Thor's relationship to his wife, Sif. Sif was known for her long, golden hair. She was a Goddess of the grain and the fields. Fertility came from a union between earth and sky, Sif being the earth and Thor being the sky. There are still folk beliefs in Scandinavian countries that fields of grain need to be struck by lightning before they are fertile. Any field struck by lightning is considered blessed by the union of Thor and Sif.

Although worship of Thor may have died out, belief in him never has. Folklorist Jacob Grimm wrote about many common folk sayings that invoked Thor's name well into the nineteenth century. This can easily be brushed off as simple country folklore, but as Witches and Pagans know, many "old wives' tales" often hold magickal or spiritual significance.

Since the Marvel movie *Thor* was released, I have noticed a clear upswing in the interest in Heathenry or Asatru, which are modern revivalist traditions of old Norse and Scandinavian practices. I actually feel this is a good thing. Remembering what is remembered lives, we know this means that these Godds need to appeal to as wide a range of people as possible.

Through modern cinema and comic books, Thor has opened the door to a whole new level of worship and attention. He has become as modern as a Godd can be. Plus, this is an entryway for people to find out more about the Old Godds, ancient traditions, and Paganism in general. I'm all for it.

And, conversely, it must also be said that there are serious threads of racism that come through some of the Heathen and Asatru modern culture. There have been groups that want to bring back the "old religion of Europe" and paint Europe with a white brush.

There isn't and never has been a "religion of Europe." Even in places where the Godds were vast and known across a wide landscape, they had their own regional flavors, styles, names, and practices. Europe never was unified and likely never will be. Also, Europe is not "white." I am totally against any religious practices that seek out the old ways as a veneer of racism, sexism, or holding up any other patriarchal bullshit.

HIS STORY

The giants beneath the sea planned a lavish banquet for all of the Gods of Asgard, but they would only be willing to host this event if the Gods could bring them a cauldron large enough to brew a mead for all who would attend. Because of the sheer size of vessel needed, it would have to be magickal. The Gods knew that only one such cauldron existed in all of the realms and it belonged to the giant, Hymir.

Giants were notorious for being difficult to deal with and many Gods were unsuccessful in handling the giants' temperamental natures. The Gods discussed the issue and all agreed that Thor should be the one to go and visit Hymir and attempt to gain the cauldron.

The plans were set in motion and Thor traveled to the house of Hymir. In order to be a hospitable host, Hymir had slaughtered three bulls to feed the mighty God. However, Thor ate two of these bulls immediately. The giant was unprepared to feed a God of Thor's hunger and felt rather upset about having to deal with the God's massive appetite. Hymir announced that they would have to go fishing the next day in order to have enough food to keep the God well-fed.

In the morning, Hymir sent Thor out to collect bait for their fishing trip. Thor proceeded to kill the largest of Hymir's prize bulls in order to use the head as bait. Hymir was quite bothered by Thor's brash and rather rude behavior. He was also increasingly worried that they would be unsuccessful in their fishing trip and the giant would have nothing to feed the red bearded God.

The two got into the boat and Thor rowed them out to the sea. Hymir immediately caught two whales and was delighted; this much food should last a while, even with Thor's appetite. But Thor kept rowing the boat out farther, deeper into the vast ocean. Hymir began to feel nervous, as they were reaching the territory of Jormungand, the dangerous sea serpent that was slowly devouring the Earth from below.

Thor only smiled a wicked grin, knowing full well where the boat was headed. His face was tight and grim, thinking of his old enemy Jormungand. He stopped the boat and dropped in his fishing line. Almost immediately there was a tug on the line. Thor started to reel it in, but the line pulled back, almost yanking him out of the boat. Thor braced himself, pulling on the line and gritting his teeth against the tension. The waves began to rock the boat and a great rumbling came from below. Thor's smile grew wider.

Hymir watched the mighty God with an increasing terror stealing over him. The giant began to protest, but Thor only pushed his feet harder against the bottom of the boat, allowing water to creep in through the cracks that the pressure of his weight was creating.

This went on for some time, until finally the giant serpent's head peeked above the waterline. Its large mouth and jagged venom-dripping teeth came alarmingly close to the side of the boat. Thor only grimaced, picking up his hammer with one hand and holding the line with the other. Hymir began to panic as the head of the sea serpent came closer and closer to the edge of the boat.

Hymir shouted in warning, but Thor ignored him, holding fast to the line. Sweat broke out on Hymir's forehead, fear shooting through his body. He jumped up, cutting the line. Immediately, there was a thud against the boat as the tension released. A roar escaped the mouth of Jormungand before it sunk back beneath the waves, swimming into the depths of the sea. As the monster escaped, a cry of frustration and rage left the mouth of Thor while he watched his greatest enemy slip through his fingers.

Thor's anger overtook him and he raised his mighty hammer to strike Hymir, but instead of killing the giant he knocked him overboard. The boat began to break apart as Thor rowed back to shore with the giant's two whales. Thor held on, riding the waves of the sea as the wood pieces splintered and broke beneath him, finally being destroyed to nothing as he reached the shore. He started to head back to Asgard, but before he left, he grabbed the great cauldron of Hymir.

Shortly upon his return, there was a great feast hosted by the giants of the deep sea with a cauldron offering enough brew to satiate all of the Gods.

THOR CORRESPONDENCES

- Lightning

- Thunder

- Storms
- Wheat
- Oak trees
- Goats
- Mead

THOR RITUAL: THE WORLD TREE

I feel closest to Thor when I am at the gym. In fact, most of my relationship with Thor is connected to physical exertion. He is a very physical Godd, which shouldn't come as a surprise seeing that he was a Godd of the warriors and working people. But this doesn't mean that you have to pump iron, be in good shape, or even work out to have a relationship with Thor. There is more to him than a strong physique. He can also help create strong boundaries, solid protective instincts, and fierce love.

The following ritual for Thor is a physical one, but it can be modified for those with varying physical needs and abilities. It is written for someone with no physical limitations, which isn't the case for most people, including myself. Please modify as needed to fit your body.

This ritual is written for a solitary practitioner, but can be easily modified for a group or coven. If working with a group, each participant will need their own offering cup.

SUPPLIES

small disposable container/offering cup

mead

SET UP

This ritual is best done if you can be in a wild place: a forest, a cliff-side, or a trail. If this isn't possible, a public park will work, but the larger the better. A place where you can feel the expanse of the sky above you and can sit below a tree is ideal.

There is no altar to build for this ritual, but you will need some mead and a small disposable container. This could be a compostable cup, but a natural object that is from the local environment is best. For example, an acorn top, a walnut husk, or a leaf big enough to hold some liquid.

RITUAL

Find the path or trail that you will be following. Before stepping onto the trail, take a moment to breathe, ground, and center yourself.

Cast a simple circle around yourself that is also portable. You will need the circle to move with you as you walk down the trail. When you feel ready, say this:

Hail Thor
I call upon you today, I invite you into this rite
I ask for your wisdom, your awareness, your fight
Hail and welcome to you, God
Great Thor, please join me now
Bring forth your power here
To grow my power, please show me how
Hail and welcome, Thor

Once this is complete, take a deep breath and let yourself be fully present. Focus your awareness. Notice where you are pulled, stuck, or distracted. Reel all of these threads of your awareness back to yourself.

Imagine these threads like little fishing lines out in the world. Unhook those places and reel these lines back in. Pull in all of the lines that are keeping your energy from being fully present. Breathe deeply, with each inhale draw in those disparate pieces of you back into your body. Draw in all of your awareness and let it gather in your third eye—that spot just above and just between your normal seeing eyes. Continue to pull in all your threads of awareness letting that ball of energy build and grow.

When that ball of awareness is full and you feel ready, let that ball begin to slowly drop down your body. Slowly push your awareness from the top of your head down your throat. Continue to push that ball of awareness down your body, through your chest, down your belly, down into your pelvic bowl. Here, at your pelvic bowl, allow this ball to come to rest.

Take a moment to notice what it feels like to have your awareness sitting in your pelvic bowl, concentrated there in that place. Breathe deeply and allow this ball of energy to slowly unfurl. Let your awareness expand just beyond the outside of your body, but keep it rooted in your pelvic bowl.

Open your eyes and look around this place in nature. See what it is like to be in this place with your awareness shifted and expanded. When you feel ready, begin to walk down the trail. There will be times when your awareness starts to lift back up or get shifted or distracted. That's okay; just take a moment to breathe and push that energy back down into your pelvic bowl.

Walk down the trail and pay attention as you do. Notice what stands out. Notice how things appear from this altered state. Walk along the trail for as long as you feel called to do so. When you feel ready, find a tree that you can sit beneath with your back against the trunk.

Keep yourself in the altered state of awareness, but also notice the awareness of the tree where you sit. Every tree is a gateway to the world tree, to Yggdrasil. Allow your awareness to shift again, pulling it back into your body and allowing it to run up and down the length of your spine. Feel the power of the tree and your own personal power running next to each other.

Feel the expansiveness of this tree. Feel how this single tree is all the worlds and holds all the worlds. Thor meets you here. In this realm between the realms, this world between the worlds. Allow space to speak with him, to explore Yggdrasil, and see what information is here for you now in this moment.

When you feel ready, say goodbye to Thor and release your awareness from Yggdrasil. Shift your awareness fully into your body and allow it to spread out, shifting back into its normal state of being. Notice your breathing and the edges of your body. Lean forward, shifting away from the tree, and tap the edges of your body. Touch the top of your head and say your name out loud.

When you are ready, slowly stand up. Look with your normal seeing eyes and take note of anything interesting. Begin to follow the path that brought you to this tree. Walk along with your normal seeing eyes back to the beginning of the trail. When you reach the trailhead, pour the libation of mead into the chosen container and set it down. State out loud that this is an offering of gratitude for Thor.

Say this:

> *Thank you, Thor*
> *For joining in this rite*
> *Thank you for your wisdom*
> *Thank you for your fight*
> *Hail and farewell to you, God*
> *Hail and farewell, Thor*

Open the circle that you created and carried with you, releasing the magick that you built and letting it dissipate back into the earth.

The work is done. Hail Thor!

LILITH

LILITH CULTURE

The Goddess Lilith has gained quite a following in modern Witchcraft and Paganism, and it's no surprise that this is the case. The transformation of Lilith from first woman to demon is a clear reflection of what was happening to the culture of the world during the time of her origin. Even now there are stories of Lilith in Jewish and Christian myth that suggest she is a demon who preys on sleeping men, seeking out their semen to increase her hoard of demon babies (Black Koltuv 1986).

From a historical perspective, it is unlikely that Lilith was the original "wife" of Adam. In fact, most evidence of Lilith's connection to Judeo-Christian myths originated in religious satire that was written by ancient Hebrews. Earlier evidence of Lilith comes from Sumer, sometime between 4000 BCE and 3100 BCE; here she is called Lilitu and is a creature that won't leave Inanna's Huluppu tree (Wolkstein 1983).

Later she shows up in Babylonian sources sometime between 2000 BCE and 1600 BCE. From this time period, there remain images of Lilith in which she has the face of a beautiful woman with bird's feet and dangerous talons. It's not until sometime between 700 BCE and 600 BCE that she starts to show up in the writings of Middle Eastern Jews as the first wife of Adam.

She is mentioned in the Alphabet of Ben Sira, which was considered religious satire. These writings demean Adam for being unable to control his first wife and further suggest that all uncontrollable women are demons. In the Hebrew language, the word *lilith* translates to "night creature" or "screech owl." It's not hard to draw the correlation between screech owl and demon woman (Black Koltuv 1986).

As time goes forward, historically the stories of Lilith demonize her more and more. She becomes the ultimate demonic power, going after men when they are most vulnerable: while they are sleeping. In these stories she coaxes men to ejaculate in their sleep so that she may steal their seed and create a great race of demonic children. She is the succubus, the seductress, with the church using her as a symbol of why men should be afraid of women's sexuality.

Her power as demoness continued to grow over the years, making her the greatest of all female demons. In writings and myth she is elevated to the consort of the king of all demons, Asmodeus. The two of them create an army of demons that haunt men and steal children. Anytime something went wrong, Asmodeus and Lilith were often to blame.

In modern times we have to look at some of the magickal power that continues to be a part of Lilith's story. She is known for her power, her connection to sexuality, her gate-keeping of the Otherworld. Modern practitioners, especially those that practice Satanism, share techniques on how to access her power and harness her energy. Even now she is exploited.

Over the last thirty years, modern Witches and Pagans have elevated Lilith to a powerful feminist being. She is honored as an entity that shows women how to speak truth to power. She demands to be respected as equal and refuses to lie beneath any man. Especially through the 1990s, Lilith's popularity with modern practitioners grew as the new contemporary feminist movement outside of Witchcraft grew as well.

HER STORY

The Great God, whose true name could not be spoken, created two beings from the mud of the earth. The first of these beings was called Adam, the first man. The second of these beings was called Lilith, the first woman. Adam and Lilith together were called husband and wife and they lived in the most beautiful garden called Eden.

Although in this paradise Lilith and Adam had all that they needed, Lilith found herself questioning the truth of their reality. Her creator had made everything so perfect. The beauty of the garden was like nothing else on earth—or so they were told. The flowers were always in bloom and they smelled so sweet. The trees had buds, blossoms, and fruit, all at the same time. The birds were small and delicate with a song that would make her weep with joy. She was never cold, never hungry, and never sad. Life in Eden was perfect.

And yet, Lilith wondered what was on the other side of the hedges. She knew that there was something else over there. At night they heard noises:

snuffling, scratching, mewling, howling. Sometimes the sounds would make the hair on her arms stand on end, but rather than fill her with fear, they made her more and more curious. She longed to know what was on the other side of the hedge. She wanted to see what else the world held, wanted to know its secrets. And she wanted to know why her Creator would not let them see. She wanted to know why they must stay locked behind the hedges.

Lilith spoke to Adam about these things, but he seemed uninterested. "Why worry about what is outside of Eden?" He would respond. "We have everything we need here."

Lilith did love Adam, but his apathy concerned her.

As time went on, their paradise began to feel like a prison. Yes, they wanted for nothing, but they also received no answers, no clarity, and had no freedom to leave. She began to feel stifled by the green hedges. The animals, plants, and creatures of Eden started to look like tricks, beautiful distractions to keep her compliant.

One afternoon, when Lilith and Adam made love, he demanded she lie beneath him. Lilith refused, stating that they were equals and should therefore lay side-by-side. Adam responded that he was created first, and was therefore superior and she should do as he commanded.

This was the last straw for Lilith. The walls of her false paradise closed in on her. Adam was a pliable thing for their Creator to use. She wanted her freedom and she possessed the power to claim that freedom, by claiming her own divinity. The way became clear to her.

To know the true name of a being is to have power over that being. Lilith knew this magick, and more importantly she knew the true name of the Creator. She spoke the true name of Yahweh, demanding her release from this beautiful prison. Her Creator, fearful of her power in speaking His name, immediately released her from Eden, banishing her from his garden paradise and locking the gates behind her. Adam was no longer her husband and Eden was no longer her home.

She wept for her husband, for she did love him. But now she took her place as Goddess, as divine being. By choosing to leave the paradise of her Creator, she became freedom, she became Goddess, she became Lilith.

Many years later, Adam would find her again and they would spend 130 years together, reunited. But by then the people had been taught that she was evil. The people feared her power because she knew the truth of Yahweh's name. She possessed the deep magick. And so their reunion was brief in the time of immortals. Adam returned to his more pliable wife, Eve, and Lilith continued on as Queen of the Demons.

LILITH CORRESPONDENCES

- Snakes
- Gardens
- Demons
- Owls
- Trees

"POEM TO LILITH" BY ALICIA FOSTER-SCALES

What they don't tell you
Is how *long* I was there
Before I chose to flee;
How long I dwelt in glass-eyed bliss
Among the grasses.
How long I followed their rules
Because I had known nothing else.
Ignorance breeds complacency, you see.
What they don't tell you is that I *knew* what I was giving up.
I was aware of what it would mean
To leave.
They don't tell you that I agonized, faltered, retreated…
And rose again.

—◆·◆·◆—

LILITH RITUAL: THE VOICE OF TRUTH

—◆·◆·◆—

Lilith chose to give up the life that she knew, the life that was comfortable and safe, in order to step into her God-self. She didn't know when she took on Yahweh and spoke his true name what was waiting for her on the other side. She didn't know that she would be made a Goddess, but she knew that she had to speak her truth. She had to stand up for herself and made the change, no matter how scary it may have been.

Of all the gifts that Lilith can bring, helping you to find your voice and speak your truth is one of the most powerful. In this ritual you will have an opportunity to connect with Lilith in your Place of Power and open your voice.

This ritual is designed for a solitary practitioner. Although it can be modified for a group or coven, it is best done alone.

SUPPLIES

red roses

representation of an owl (statue, figurine, or picture)

an image or statue of Lilith

one large red candle

sweet cakes

wine (juice or water can be used)

a goblet

an offering bowl

a bowl of salt

myrrh incense

frankincense incense

broom

bell

athame

SET UP

On your altar, place a vase of red roses or flowers, a representation of an owl, an image or statue of Lilith, a large red candle, sweet cakes, a bottle of wine, a goblet, an offering bowl, a bowl of salt, myrrh and frankincense incense, a broom, a bell, and your athame. Arrange these items in a way that is pleasing to you.

RITUAL

Start with a cleansing bath. When you enter the ritual space, pick up the broom and sweep out the area. When this is complete, light the incense and walk it around the ritual space, starting in the farthest corner and spiraling inward, in a deosil direction. Set the lit incense down and keep it burning throughout the entire ritual.

Pick up the bowl of salt and use it to create a circle around your ritual space. Set down the salt and pick up your athame. Point your athame toward the ground and draw up some of the molten earth energy onto the blade of your athame. Drag this energy toward the north and throw it out, making an energetic barrier for your working. Draw an invoking pentacle and say this:

By the Earth that is the garden.

Continue to push this energy out as you turn to the east. Draw an invoking pentacle and say this:

By the Air that is the voice of power.

Draw your circle, turning to the south. Draw an invoking pentacle and say this:

> *By the Fire that is fierceness.*

Again turn, continuing your circle, to the west. Draw an invoking pentacle and say this:

> *By the Water that is transformation.*

Turn again to face the north to complete your circle and draw
another invoking pentacle. Move to the center of your ritual space,
pointing your athame above you, and draw an invoking pentacle.
Say:

> *By all the stars above.*

Point your athame downward, drawing an invoking pentacle,
and say:

> *By the red star below. The circle is cast. I am
> between the worlds and what happens between the
> worlds changes all the worlds. Blessed be.*

Face the altar, raise your hands up in the Goddess pose, and say
this:

> *Lilith, fierce one*
> *Lilith, brave one*
> *Lilith, bloodthirsty*
> *Lilith, demoness*
> *Lilith, I call to you*
> *Lilith, into this circle you are bid*

Lilith, your powerful spirit
Lilith, your unflinching truth
Lilith, be here now

On these last words, bring your hands down to your sides and light the red candle. Sit in front of the altar and chant Lilith's name. Continue to chant her name over and over again until you feel her presence in the ritual space.

Allow yourself to be comfortable; sit or lie down. Record the following trance and listen back. Start with the trance induction.

TRANCE

Open your inner eye and find yourself at the door that leads to the center of your Place of Power. Knock three times and enter, stepping out into your place. Survey your surroundings and chant Lilith's name three times. Look again into the distance and watch for a trail or path that calls to you. As soon as a path becomes clear, begin to walk toward it.

Take notice of this path, what kind of scenery passes by as you follow it. Take note of any interesting sights, smells, or noises along the path. Place one foot in front of the other, step by step, following this path to Lilith. (Pause...) Ahead of you is running water and a sandy shoreline holding in the sides of a swiftly flowing river. As you move closer to this water the path turns sandy and you can hear the crunch of it underfoot. The scent of dampness and rotting things hits your nose as you walk along the bank.

Down the bank of the shore you see a creature drinking water. From the distance it looks like a large, terrifying bird with the head of a woman and long, flowing dark hair. But as you move closer the being shifts, changing position, and the form of a woman stands up turning toward you. It is Lilith.

She begins to walk toward you while beckoning you to come closer at the same time. You move a foot forward, step by step coming closer and closer to this Goddess. When you reach each other, Lilith speaks. Take some time to hear her words of wisdom for you and ask the questions you hold about using your voice (Pause).

After your questions have been asked, Lilith lifts her hand to your throat. A light emanates from her palm and something shifts into place in your throat. It is a feeling of clearing, clarity, and truth. She smiles, releasing you and pulling her energy back.

Your time here in this realm is limited. Take a moment to offer your gratitude to Lilith and say goodbye. (Pause) Although you must leave from here for now, you have found the path to Lilith and can return here at any time.

Lilith returns to the edge of the river as you turn to move back onto the trail that brought you here. Let your feet carry you closer and closer to the center of your Place of Power. Your feet move, one foot in front of the other. Step by step you move down the path, back to the center of your PoP. Again, take notice of any sights, smells, or sounds that come to you as you walk.

The path clears and again you step into the center of your Place of Power. Take a moment to anchor anything from this experience that needs to be grounded here. Go back to your doorway and step through. As you do so, close your inner eye. Allow yourself to shift back into this time and place.

Notice your breathing. Take some time to slowly reconnect with your body. Slowly open your eyes and take a look around your ritual space. Tap the edges of your body and say your name out loud three times. Take a moment to write down anything pertinent or important from your trance journey.

Sit in front of your altar and speak the things that you have been unable to say. Say out loud the things that have been stuck in your throat. If nothing comes, just allow yourself to make noise, groan, tone, grunt, or speak, letting any words fall out of you that need to. If nothing comes at all, go back to chanting Lilith's name.

Let this continue for some time. Let your voice get louder and softer as you feel called. Let yourself sing, scream, chant, and make whatever noises at whatever tempo or timbre your body wants to make them. When you feel complete, bring yourself back into silence and stillness for some time. When you begin to feel uncomfortable, take three deep breaths.

Pour wine into the glass. Use your athame to draw a pentacle over the top of the glass three times and say this:

> By the power of three times three, this
> wine is blessed, so mote it be!

Pour some of the wine into the offering bowl, and as you do, say this:

> Wine given to Lilith, in gratitude,
> in graciousness, with grace.

Take a moment to drink some of the wine. Drink it slowly. Relish in feeling it flow down your throat. Really allow yourself to taste this drink. Feel how it is to swallow and have your throat touched by the softness and silkiness of the wine.

Take your athame and draw a pentacle three times over the cakes. As you do, say this:

> By the power of three times three,
> this food is blessed, so mote it be!

Place one of the sweet cakes in the offering bowl. As you do, say this:

> Sweets given to Lilith, in gratitude,
> in graciousness, with grace.

Make space to speak to Lilith from your heart. Say anything else that still needs to be said. Offer any gratitude or appreciation you feel. When you feel complete, stand up, raise your hands into a Goddess pose, and say this:

Lilith, fierce one
Lilith, brave one
Lilith, bloodthirsty
Lilith, demoness
Lilith, I thank you for bringing
your powerful spirit
your unflinching truth
Lilith, hail and farewell

Extinguish the red candle. Pick up your athame and point it to the ground. Draw a banishing pentacle below you; release the red star fire energy that you used to build your sacred space. Say this:

I release the red star below.

Point your athame above you and draw a banishing pentacle, then say this:

I release the stars above.

Point your athame to the north and slice open your container as you move widdershins to the west. Draw a banishing pentacle and say this:

Thank you, Water, that is transformation.

Turn toward the south, slicing open the circle as you move. Face the south, draw a banishing pentacle, and say:

Thank you, Fire, that is fierceness.

Turn toward the east, slicing open the circle as you move. Face the east and say this:

Thank you, Air, that is the voice of power.

Turn toward the north, releasing the final piece of your circle. Face the north and say this:

Thank you, Earth, that is the garden.

Say this:

The circle is open, but unbroken.
Hail Lilith. Merry we shall meet again.

The work is done! Hail Lilith!

OTHER GODDS OF REVOLUTION

Medusa: Greek, Goddess of regeneration and righteous anger

Artemis: Greek, Goddess of the hunt

Rhiannon: Welsh, Goddess of sovereignty

Oya: Afro-Caribbean, Goddess of change

Brigantia: Celtic, Goddess of victory

Cathubodua: Gaulish, Goddess of battle

The Morrigan: Irish, Goddess of battle

Baubo: Greek, Goddess of humor and liberation

Kali: Hindu, Goddess of destruction

Mayari: Tagalog, Goddess of war and revolution

Liberty: Roman, Goddess of freedom and revolution

Prometheus: Greek, Godd of subversive acts

Uranus: Greek, primal Godd of heaven and the sky

Section Two

HONOR

7

ANCESTORS

Talking about the dead from a Pagan context is rather difficult. We Pagans don't have one dogma on what happens after we die. In Paganism you will find folks who believe in reincarnation, Valhalla, going to an ancestral realm, going into a cosmic realm, heaven, or absolutely nothing—when you're dead, you're dead. Plus, Pagans can believe any and all of these things at once.

I'm not going to give you a clear and definitive answer on what happens after death. I believe that death is the greatest mystery of being human. However, I will say that no matter what you feel happens after death, there are many ways to work with the dead, with the ancestors, and with those that have crossed over.

In many esoteric schools of thought, especially Hermeticism, there is a concept called the Law of Paradox. The depth and complication of this rule can (and likely will) be argued about until the end of times. But at its most simple core, the Law of Paradox is this: two things in opposition of each other can both be true. The truth of one does not negate the truth of the other. Basically, life is not black and white. Rules are not a simple this or that. The world is much more complex than we can even fathom.

I use the Law of Paradox to bring some sort of resolution into my own feelings about life after death. The Law of Paradox allows me to believe that after death we can simultaneously reincarnate, have a spirit body that stays behind to help descendants, go to Valhalla, and/or have it all just end. I'm totally okay with this.

Even with all of these vast and varying ideas on death, most Pagan traditions hold a practice of honoring the ancestors. Simply put, the ancestors are the folks that came before us. We honor them and give them reverence because they made our lives possible—literally. The ancestors are our lineage going all the way back to the beginning of humanity. The ancestors made our lives possible. In honoring the ancestors we honor ourselves, by recognizing that our lives could not be possible without the work of those that came before. The ancestors are the easiest to connect with because they are a part of us.

Moving forward in this book, I will address the dead in three categories. The first is the ancestors. These are the dead of our lineage, of blood, birth, and adoption. The second is the Beloved Dead. These are the people that we loved, bonded with, admired, or forged relationships with that may not have been family or relatives. The Beloved Dead may be friends, community members, lovers, friends, pets, famous people, and anyone that impacted us. The third are the Mighty Dead—also referred to as the Mighty Dead of the Craft. These are specifically the dead of our Witch and Pagan lineage. Sometimes the Mighty Dead were well known in their time; but more often than not, the names of the Mighty Dead are unknown to us.

Before we go any further, it is important for me to say this: you don't have to work with or acknowledge an ancestor that was abusive or harmful. Just because someone has died doesn't mean that they are automatically enlightened or clear on all the wrong they did in life. I've heard spiritual fallacy that in order to be good spiritual practitioners we have to forgive those that harmed us and move on. This is plain false. You don't have to forgive anyone, and that doesn't mean that you're not "spiritual enough." There are plenty of ancestors in your lineage. Don't feel like you are forced to work with some asshole that was abusive.

Ancestor work can also be difficult for those folks who don't know their ancestry because they don't have relationships with their blood relations. This also doesn't prevent you from working with ancestors. Adoptive family ancestors are your ancestors. And thanks to modern technology we have the ability to have our DNA tested and find out about our blood origins. Getting a DNA test can be especially revealing for ancestral work, even if you think you know all about your familial origins. You don't have to know the names of your ancestors in order to have relationships with them.

> *Note: There is controversy about DNA testing. There are debates on how accurate the testing process is. There are also debates on the security of providing your DNA to a large company. I have had my DNA tested and found it to be very revealing for my personal work, but this may not be the case for everyone. There are ways to connect to your ancestors without DNA information.*

Healing yourself heals your bloodline, going both forward and backward. You don't have to know your ancestors to do this work. You don't have to like your ancestors to do this work. But for your own sake and the sake of your descendants you *should* do this work. When I speak of the descendants I am referring to the children you may bring to life from your bloodline, the children you may nurture, the relationships you foster with love, and any Witches or Pagans that you bring into the fold. Your descendants will be those who remember you after you pass on.

The way I look at ancestral lineage is a simplistic one. Although we all have vast and complex family trees where we may be able to trace our bloodlines, we can't really comprehend much further than our four main threads of ancestry.

What I mean by four bloodlines are the four grandparents of your immediate family ancestry—your parent's parents. This can be difficult for folks who have no connection with their parents or grandparents of blood, but the way we understand the concept is the same, whether we know these people or not.

Our minds have a hard time holding the more complex pattern of ancestry beyond our four grandparents. If we look past our generation to our parents, we shift from looking at ourselves as singlular, to the product of two individuals. If we stretch that one step further, we move from the pair (our parents, as two individuals) to a lineage of four, our grandparents.

It's not uncommon to have no relationship with grandparents. It's not uncommon to have lost grandparents before ever having a chance to talk with them about their lives, history, and genealogy. Many of our grandparents had to give up some of their ancestral lineage due to immigration, war, or other difficult circumstances. However, if we can connect to these four threads we can get a clearer picture of who we are, even if it's only two generations back.

In my lineage, I know my maternal line pretty clearly. My grandmother was born in France to French parents. I know my ancestry in that bloodline goes back to France. Beyond that it gets murky. My grandfather was born on the East Coast of the United States with a Dutch name. His ancestry is even murkier. I've got some muddy ideas of German and Dutch heritage, but not much more. However, learning about French and Dutch traditions in my lineage allows me to fill in a bit of the picture about myself.

On the other side, my father's mother's bloodline goes back in the United States to 1776. I was able to trace that thanks to Ancestry.com. My grandfather by blood was not the man I knew to be my grandfather for most of my life. Only when I got older did I learn about the man who was my blood. He was born in the United States, but most of his siblings were born in Norway. And with that piece of information, another blank is filled in.

Beyond these four threads it is hard to be sure. The branches of our family trees grow exponentially, doubling with each generation. The further back you go, the harder it is to have clarity. And so it becomes a practice of trust, patience, and faith. Even if you have a family tree that has been carefully collected and curated for generations, there is still a level of uncertainty and an inability to fully grock what it all means.

Through the process of bloodlines, lineage, and ancestor work, let yourself be open to possibility. Let yourself be open to exploration. Let yourself be open to surprises.

Working with the ancestors can be done on the macro level, by looking at your cultural lineages without specifics—like "the Vikings." And it can also be done looking at the micro level, by finding a specific name from your bloodline and seeking that individual out. You may also discover that as you open yourself up to ancestor work, you may encounter someone you've never heard of and cannot even prove existed. It's all okay.

The digging into ancestry can also be painful. Learning about the heroes and villains in your bloodline can be shocking. Learning about the suffering your ancestors experienced can be heartbreaking. It has been proven that we carry these ancestral wounds with us. The harm that happened to our ancestors is still carried in our bones and blood. This is the hard work of it, but it also gives us a chance to do some healing and take our ancestral power back.

Learning about the cultures that I am descended from has given me a new perspective on my own life. I have been able to connect to the Godds from the lands of my ancestors, only to discover how wonderfully happy they were that I was reaching out. My ancestors of blood served as a bridge to help me connect more deeply to my ancient Pagan roots.

I don't know many of their names, but that doesn't really matter. I have been able to discover the names of towns that they lived in, folklore and myth from some of these regions, and customs that my family carries on today without remembering why or where they originated. It is a blessing that technology can connect us to the power of our own bloodline.

ANCESTOR RITUAL

This ritual can be done at any time when you want to honor or connect to your ancestors. This ritual will have peak efficacy if done during Samhain-tide (from the Fall Equinox to the Winter Solstice). It is written for a solitary practitioner, but it can be easily modified for a group.

SET UP

Pull out items that are sacred to your ancestors. These items may already be on an ancestor altar: dishes, jewelry, ritual items, books, linens, ashes, and so on. You will be creating a large altar, so use what you've got. Don't put the altar together, just have all of the items ready to go.

Spend the day leading up to the ritual cooking food that was favored by the ancestors that you will be working with. If you are planning to honor many ancestors from many different places, this may require some serious advanced planning.

If you don't have any items that may have belonged to your ancestors or know of their favorite foods or regional foods, don't let that stop you. If you know anything about your heritage, choose colors or items that may be culturally significant. If you don't know anything about your lineage, choose items that are significant to you personally. How would you set an altar or sacred space to reflect who you are? Pick items that are special and unique to you and your practice. Do the same with foods. What are your favorite foods, what would you cook for a dinner party?

Remember, you are the current member of your ancestry and lineage. What you love and deem special and important will be significant for your descendants. Ancestry runs backward, but it also runs forward. You can introduce yourself to your ancestors through your own beloved items.

SUPPLIES

sacred items, decorations, fabrics of your choice

frankincense incense

fireproof container

wand or athame

plate

goblet

paper and pen

SET UP

Before you do anything else, take a moment to burn the frankincense and blow the smoke across your altar space as a way to cleanse it. On your altar, place your wand or athame, a plate, a goblet, three candles, a paper and pen, a fireproof bowl, and more frankincense incense.

Take a cleansing bath and anoint yourself with an oil or perfume that you love. Dress in nice clothes and begin the ritual.

RITUAL

Ground and center yourself to prepare fully for the rite. Allow yourself to become fully present. Pick up your athame or wand and create sacred space in your favorite way. If you have been trained or initiated in a specific lineage, cast the circle in the way of your training.

Take the items that you have set aside and create an elaborate altar space. Use the family items, fabrics, and other decorations that appeal to you and make you think of your ancestors. You can always add in some of your other ritual items, fresh flowers, or other decorations that appeal to you.

Call your ancestors into your ritual space. Say this:

> *I call to you, ancestors. Those who have gone before.*
> *Ancestors of my lineage, ancestors of breath, blood,*
> *and bone. Ancestors who have made my life possible.*
> *I call to you and welcome you to this rite.*

Name as many names as you want to call into the circle.

Pour a libation into the goblet on the altar; this can be wine, juice, tea, coffee, water, or spirits. Sit in front of the altar and write a letter to your ancestors. Explain to them why you are performing this ritual. Ask for their counsel, advice, or inspiration. Let them know that you are open to learning more about your lineage. Tell them what you hope to gain from a deeper connection with them.

When complete, read the letter out loud and then burn it in your fireproof container. If there is a concern about smoke, burn the letter outdoors. Use the ashes to anoint yourself, touching them to your third eye, throat, and heart. Sit in silent meditation or contemplation. Allow yourself to just be present with the ancestors that you have called in. See if any information or messages come through and write them down to look at later. Don't try to process anything in the moment.

Take out the food and put the first serving of each dish on the plate on the altar. Serve yourself afterward, and then eat with your ancestors.

When you are finished, thank your ancestors. Start by naming all that you called into the space. Say this:

> *Thank you, ancestors, for joining my rite. Ancestors*
> *of my lineage, ancestors of breath, blood, and bone,*
> *thank you. Ancestors who made my life possible,*

whose shoulders I now stand on, thank you. May
our work continue together, but from this circle. Hail
and farewell.

Open your circle in your favorite way or in the way you were trained in your lineage. Leave the altar space up for as long as possible, taking it down before the Winter Solstice.

8

BELOVED DEAD

The Beloved Dead can be the hardest and potentially most painful of all the relationships with the dead we may foster. The Beloved Dead are those that we loved in life. They may be relatives of your blood, but they could just as easily be friends, teachers, mentors, lovers, famous people, children, or pets. Not only do we have to process grief with our Beloved Dead, but our memories and histories with them will color our relationships with them when they cross over.

When a beloved dies, we can hold expectation that they should visit us, connect with us, or show up and let us know it's all okay for them. Sometimes this does happen, but it isn't always the case. Since we can't fully know what happens when someone dies, we can't fully know what a spirit needs to do when they first cross over.

In working with the Beloved Dead, we may crave connection with them. Grief can make us desperate or angry. We may deeply desire any scrap of connection with our Beloved Dead. We may be angry or broken with loss, and this can color any potential connection. Grief, anger, desperation, or any other emotion isn't wrong or bad; you are fully allowed to feel and experience a wide range of emotions. However, it is important to be aware that the freshness of loss can make it difficult for the Beloved Dead to connect. Sometimes time is needed.

There are a lot of superstitions about working with the Beloved Dead, and many traditions have different rules, so your mileage on this may vary. Generally speaking, it is believed that there is some amount of time that should be given to someone who has crossed over before you start to call on them as an ally. The reason for this is because they may have their own work to do before they will be ready to lend their aid to the living. The appropriate timeline varies greatly from one tradition to the next. Some traditions suggest waiting thirty days, while others wait as long as a year to three years.

It is typical to call on the Beloved Dead at Samhain-tide. In the Reclaiming Tradition we speak the names of our Beloved Dead of that year with the blessing "what is remembered lives." This happens at Samhain because, as Witches and Pagans, this is when we believe the veil between the worlds is the thinnest. This is the time of the year when our dead can connect with us most easily.

We speak their names in ritual for two reasons. The first is to honor them. The transition from life to death is a great mystery. We want to honor those that have stepped through and into that mystery. The second reason is purely human: we need to grieve. Grief is powerful, cleansing, and important. To grieve our Beloved Dead in public or with others is healing. Taking the honoring and emotion of loss from the privacy of our individual experience into a community experience is a revolutionary act. What is remembered lives!

GRIEF AS A MAGICKAL PRACTICE

It is said that there are five stages of grief. These stages were made famous by Elisabeth Kübler-Ross in her book *On Death and Dying*, with the ideas being further explored in her book written with David Kessler, *On Grief and Grieving*. These concepts have become a part of mainstream psychology in dealing with the death of a loved one. And the fact that the grieving process is laid out in five simple to follow stages does nothing to really clarify the grief process.

It is not a simple path to follow. It is not linear. It does not move from here to there. Grief is a complicated thing, twisting and turning over itself.

The five stages don't really move in order. You may find that you have moved into the stage of depression over a loss, only to find yourself pushed "backward" into the stage of anger. Rather than thinking of these steps as a map that leads from one step to the next, I think of them like a guidebook. The stages can help you sort out where you are and how you might best pronounce your grief, hold it, or move through it.

And the harshest truth is that the grief process never stops, but it shifts into a place where we can find some semblance of peace with what has happened. It may never feel okay. It may be a wound that never heals, but life and time continues to move forward and so must we.

There are a lot of shortcomings in the concept of the five stages of grief, but they can be made into a magickal practice to help process the death of a Beloved.

+ **Denial:** Simply stated, this is the initial point. The "I can't believe it" phase. During the denial phase you may find yourself convinced that there has been a mistake or it's been some sort of terrible joke. Even when a death is expected, this denial can be a part of the grieving process. It is a state of shock when the reality of the loss is just too big to fully process.

+ **Anger:** This emotion can be directed virtually anywhere and at anyone. Perhaps you are angry with your dead, with yourself, with the medical establishment, with the Godds. Anger can be a cap holding back other emotions. The best way to deal with anger is to fully experience it and allow it to come through in healthy ways.

+ **Bargaining/Guilt:** At some point you will find yourself making deals with a higher power to bring your loved one back. This can also manifest as looking at all the "what ifs." Looking at all the choices and opportunities when you could have done something differently. When you may have had a chance of saving your loved one, even if there really was no chance of that.

+ **Depression:** Eventually the emptiness of the loss will hit. Most of us are familiar with what depression looks or feels like. Nothing matters, nothing is interesting, and nothing brings any ounce of joy. Living loved ones may try to rush shifting out of this stage. Attempts may be made to help someone in depression "cheer up." Although these attempts may be offered from a loving or helpful place, depression will take the time it takes. And if it does deepen into a clinical depression, medical and/or psychological help may be needed.

+ **Acceptance:** This is far from being alright and moving forward like nothing happened; acceptance is more like an understanding, a comfort with the discomfort of it. Grief never goes away, but it does dull, soften, and ease. Even when acceptance comes, there will be times, even years later, when one of the other stages rears its ugly head.

Working with grief, ritualizing grief, isn't just a one-time, fix-it-all situation. Rituals to hold grief, process it, and move through it may be done over and over again. There isn't a simple bandage that you can place on the wound of grief, but you can apply the balm of ritual to help you process what words may not be able to do alone.

Keeping a journal just for your grieving practice can help you to clear up some of your feelings, express places where you may feel stuck, and give you a sounding board for your feelings. You don't ever have to read back what you've written, unless you feel it will be helpful to your process. You could have a whole ritual where you burn the journal and release your grief.

Give your grief a name, an image, a story. Draw what your grief looks like, but remember grief isn't the enemy. Work on creating grief as an ally helping you through the process of loss. By naming your grief and giving it space in your life, you can work with it, speak with it, ask it for space, or blame it when things get difficult.

As you deal with your grief magickally you may find old unrelated wounds feeling fresh again. The loss from a decade ago, the loss from your child-hood—loss and death never fully heal. Allow the old losses to show them-selves, feel the feelings, and know that all grief is a part of the healing process. All of it helps to move you forward.

Create something in the name of your Beloved. This could be a memo-rial bench in your favorite park, a brick in a wall of remembrance, a tree, or a plaque in a spot you both loved. Of course, a gravesite also works for this. By creating a physical marker, you and others can visit to make space for grief. Allow the unveiling of that remembrance to be a ritual when you invite others to hold space and share their stories and love.

The following is a personal prayer, mantra or chant that can be used as needed through the grieving process.

> *I have the right to grieve the death of my loved one.*
> *This will happen on my own timeline.*
> *I have the right to my feelings.*
> *Others will not determine what*
> *my grieving should look like.*
> *I may demonstrate my feeling in my*
> *own healthy ways.*
> *I have the right to repeat the grieving stages.*
> *My grief only means what I want*
> *and need it to mean.*
> *This place is only temporary.*

ANCESTRAL ELEVATION

In many spiritual traditions there is a belief that the living need to help raise up our ancestors so that they may do good works on the other side. Hopefully they will do that good work to help us. The following ritual is referred to as an ancestral elevation, and one of its origins is from Kardecian Spiritism, but it is also a common practice in many Afro-Caribbean traditions.

This ritual takes nine days to complete and, depending on your success rate, it may need to be repeated. Ideally, this work is done to help those who had a difficult death. It can help them move on to the next realm and not stay on this plane as what Buddhists refer to as "hungry ghosts." Dead who had a difficult death or a lot of unfinished business may find it harder to move on. These are the dead that can cause trouble for the living and interfere in our lives in negative ways.

This ritual is done by literally lifting objects connected to your ancestors up a set of stairs. This can be done on an actual staircase or ladder, but you can create your own staircase (or tower) with large and sturdy books or bricks. The point is to lift them from the ground up a step for nine days, elevating them.

SUPPLIES

white cloth

staircase, ladder, books, or bricks

glass of water

white candle anointed with Ancestor Water

frankincense

incense burner

photo of Beloved Dead (if possible)

white flowers

SET UP

For this ritual you will need a white cloth, a staircase, a glass of water, a white candle that has been anointed with your Ancestor

Water (This is ritually charged water to help you connect to your ancestral bonds. A full recipe is on page 178.) and frankincense with an incense burner. You will need a photo of your Beloved Dead or a paper with their name, birth date, and death date written on it. You may also want to add white flowers.

RITUAL

Light the incense and let it burn while you set up the space. If you are using books or bricks you will need to be creative in how you set them up to resemble a staircase. This may take more than eight or nine books. Place the white cloth over the top. Put the cup of water on the first step, along with the picture and white candle. Light the candle and say the name of your Beloved Dead out loud.

Enter into prayer, asking for your ancestors, guides, and spiritual allies to help the spirit of this departed Beloved. Take your time and speak from your heart. When you feel complete, you may want to end your prayer with something that would have been special to your Beloved Dead. This may be a religious prayer, a poem, or a psalm. Take your time with this process. Remember that you are helping your Beloved Dead to "see the light" and move on.

When you feel finished, extinguish the candle and leave everything in place overnight. The next day come back and completely dismantle the altar space that you have created, then reassemble it. This time, place the water, candle, and picture on the second step. Follow the same process that you used the previous night. Share your prayers and be honest and open in your expression. Snuff the candle and leave the altar up overnight.

Follow this same process of setting up the altar, completing the ritual, leaving it overnight, and dismantling it in the morning, until the picture, candle, and water reach the very top step. Let this last step sit overnight and then the next day, take the altar down for the final time. Place the photo or name paper on your ancestor altar and keep it there. Ritually discard any remains, including the candle, the water, and the flowers you may have used.

To discard the remains, take any flowers or water to a crossroads and leave then. Allow the remaining candle to burn until it is complete. Bury any bits of wax that are left over. If your candles are encased in glass, recycle the glass.

Traditionally, it is recommended to do a divination on this ritual in order to see how successful the progress may have been. You can use any form of divination that you prefer: tarot, runes, cowrie shells, etc. If the divination points to more work being needed, give it a week and then start the ritual again. If the divination points to a successful working, congratulations.

9

MIGHTY DEAD

The Mighty Dead or the Mighty Dead of the Craft are those that practiced magick in their lives. When they walked the Earth they were Witches, Pagans, healers, and teachers. They may be ancestors of blood, lineage, or study. They may be people who trained us at their homes or famous writers that we've never met, but inspired us in our Witchcraft.

These individuals not only practiced the art of the Craft, but they shared their skills and knowledge with others. They shared what they knew. For many points across the globe and over the years, teaching Witchcraft was a revolutionary act. Those that were brave enough to step up and potentially put their lives at risk understood how important the Craft is. They knew it needed to live on.

There are famous Mighty Dead, just like there are "big name Pagans" presently. But there are also plenty of Mighty Dead that may only be known to Witches in their lineage. And there are even more Mighty Dead that are not known at all, whose names have disappeared over time. When we honor the Mighty Dead we honor all of those who brought Witchcraft and Paganism forward into the present.

We have ancient Witches, esoteric philosophers, midwives, herb wives, heretics, alchemists, priestesses, ecologists, and more that have all held a thread of what modern Witchcraft looks like today. The Mighty Dead are easy to connect with because they live in the lineage of the Craft. Their energy flows in the river of magick.

We call them into our rituals, we may hear their names and understand their connections, but how many of us know who the modern Mighty Dead of the Craft truly are? This is a question that is impossible to answer, because Witches and Pagans have a hard time agreeing on anything. So I've put together a very small list of some of our progenitors. These are modern Witches and Pagans whose influence on the Craft is clear and still very much present.

It was difficult to pick the handful of Witches to include in this section. As a Reclaiming Witch there was a part of me that wanted to write about leaders and Mighty Dead from my own community, like Raven Moonshadow, who did so much to build Reclaiming, but will never be known beyond the San Francisco Bay Area Reclaiming Community.

When it comes to the Mighty Dead it is imperative that we ask our teachers and elders who to honor. Who are the Mighty Dead of your own traditions? Who taught the folks that you learned from, and who taught *them?* Ask your mentors for the names of those who have crossed over that you might never have had a chance to meet. Ask your elders in the Craft to tell you stories of those that came before. Hear the stories of your teacher's teachers, and as you move forward and begin to share your knowledge and experience with others, share these stories too.

The only way to connect to the Mighty Dead is to learn about them. Read their books. Read books that others have written about them. Learn their lineage from origins to now. Who is still practicing their traditions? Just like learning the history of a deity is important to understand the depth of that Godd, understanding the history of the Mighty Dead gives understanding to the lineage of modern Witchcraft.

At this point in the evolution of Witchcraft and Paganism we have a weird extra layer we have to work through. In the early days of the modern Witchcraft movement, there was an expectation of lineage. Some of the first modern Pagans, Wiccans, and Witches made up a lot of stuff. Good stuff! Stuff that we still practice today, but make it up they did.

Some of the lineage stories or initiation tales of these old school practitioners are quite fanciful. As a naturally skeptical Witch, I find some of the origin tales to be utterly fabricated, but I know and respect many Witches who don't doubt or argue the validity of any of the tales. Ultimately, I think this is due to an evolution of our traditions. The progenitor of a tradition needed to have a fantastic tale, or long family lineage of Witchcraft, or a random meeting with a fairy being in the wood, or a romantic coven that brought them in and shared all their secrets. In the beginning of this modern revival, this fanciful origin tale gave more levity than "I made all this up."

These stories *were* needed—once upon a time—to bring validity to these early days practitioners. The idea of being initiated into the Witch mysteries by a fairy in the woods is a much more romantic and captivating story than "I was initiated by my friend in their living room one night after we drank too much." The stories of origins have become myth themselves. I tend to doubt many origin tales of some of our first practitioners, but I appreciate the web of beauty and magick that they weave for us to connect to.

The Mighty Dead want us to reach out. They want to connect. In some cases they want the opportunity to continue to teach and pass on their legacies. Those who took on leadership in life, bringing new Witches and practitioners into the fold, are likely to continue to do that work even after they have crossed over.

GERALD GARDNER (1884–1964)

No matter how you feel about the man, much of what modern Witchcraft looks like is because of Gerald Gardner and what he created and brought to the world. Gardner claimed initiation into a lineage of Witchcraft that originated in Britain. His claims to lineage are tenuous at best, and we could argue for days over the validity of those statements. But whether or not he was initiated into a line of traditional Witchcraft is actually irrelevant, because what came from him is a line of lore, practice, and study, which has survived since the 1930s (or the 1940s, depending on what you believe). This tradition is referred to as Gardnerian Wicca and it has influenced modern Wicca and Witchcraft in general.

There was much intrigue and in-fighting in those early days of the rebirth of Witchcraft and the birth of Wicca. When England repealed the laws against Witchcraft, it seems that many people wanted to be the first to publish about these secret lineages. Some of the stories put the modern Witch wars to shame with the venom and backstabbing that took place in those early days. It seems that we Witches have been arguing about whose tradition is older, Witchier, and "realer" since the beginning of our revival.

Around 1938, Gardner became involved with the Rosicrucian Order and this is likely where he met several of his future coven mates. He claimed to have been initiated at the home of Dorothy Clutterbuck, a traditional Witch, in 1939, at the age of fifty-five. But who exactly initiated him is a mystery. (Heselton 2012)

Crowley, the Golden Dawn, the Freemasons, Rosicrucian, the Key of Solomon, and other esoteric fraternities of the time have all had clear impact on Wicca as created by Gardner. And, more importantly, Wiccan ritual has greatly impacted the wider scope of modern Wicca, Witchcraft, and Paganism. Things like casting a circle, calling on the guardians of the watchtowers, the pentagram ritual, the elemental associations, and magickal tools are a combination of all of these older or contemporary traditions to Gardner's time.

Whatever Gardner may have learned from his initiation into Traditional Wicca was only in fragments, which he was very open about. He took great liberties in filling in the gaps with other esoteric traditions. What is clear is that Gardner, although devoted to esoteric study, was also interested in seeking fame. This lead to several issues for him with coven mates, including the loss of his friend and High Priestess, Doreen Valiente, from their working group. The truth of the times will never be known fully, but what remains clear is that Gardner was interested in the occult and esoteric for most of his life. What he created still maintains a long line of devotees looking to connect to Witchcraft and lineage.

I realised that I had stumbled upon something
interesting; but I was half-initiated before the
word, 'Wica' which they used hit me like a thun-
derbolt, and I knew where I was, and that the Old
Religion still existed. And so I found myself in the
Circle, and there took the usual oath of secrecy,
which bound me not to reveal certain things.
—GERALD GARDNER, *THE MEANING OF*
WITCHCRAFT,

DION FORTUNE (1890–1946)

Violet Mary Firth was the given name of the woman who would become known as Dion Fortune. Fortune lived in England her entire life, and during that time she was a known and outspoken occultist, psychic, and contemporary of Aleister Crowley. Best known for coining the phrase to describe magick as *"the art of causing changes to occur in consciousness,"* Dion is a clear foremother of modern Witchcraft practices.

Interested in the occult and psychic phenomenon for most of her young life, Fortune studied occultism and in 1919 initiated into the Order of the Golden Dawn. Soon after her initiation she transferred to a lodge led by Miona MacGregor Mathers, wife of MacGregor Mathers, one of the founders of The Golden Dawn. After years of study and disappointment in the leadership of several spiritual groups, Fortune founded the Community of Inner Light in Glastonbury, which is still in existence today.

Fortune was a prolific writer, with many books that are still considered source material for modern Witchcraft and Paganism. Her books, both fiction and nonfiction, are highly popular within magickal communities. *The Sea Priestess*, a work of fiction, is often described as one of the most beautiful books of poetry on magick ever written.

Dion Fortune believed that she was able to make contact with the Ascended Masters and that much of her writings were drawn from teachings she received from them. One of her books, *The Cosmic Doctrine*, was channeled by

Fortune in 1922 from several Ascended Masters. In 1930, Fortune decided it was time to step down from formal leadership and public life and focus more closely on her personal spiritual pursuits. Her focus during this time shifted from channeling the Ascended Masters to performing personal rituals.

After the end of the Second World War, Fortune envisioned a coming of an "Age of Aquarius." Although she didn't live to see it, we can look back and see that she wasn't far off. In her desire to help usher in this coming age, she began working on bringing the various occult and Spiritualist groups of England together. Her goal was to pool together their various resources and esoteric information.

Fortune became a prominent leader in the occult community at a time when women were unlikely to have major leadership roles. However, she is also a product of her time, holding seriously restrained ideas about sex and sexuality. Fortune brings a feminine perspective of the occult world that was dominated by men during an age when Paganism and Witchcraft of the modern version was truly being created. Her influence on modern practices can be seen in rituals today.

The Order suffered severely during the First World War, and Mathers himself died in Paris from influenza during the epidemic. When I came in touch with his organization, it was manned mainly by widows and grey-beard ancients, and did not appear to be a very promising field of occult endeavor. But I had considerable experience of practical occultism before I made its acquaintance, and I immediately recognized power of a degree and kind I had never met before, and had not the slightest doubt that I was on the trail of the genuine tradition, despite its inadequate exposition.

—Dion Fortune, Applied Magic

VICTOR ANDERSON (1917–2001)
AND CORA ANDERSON (1915–2008)

Yes, Victor and Cora are two separate people, but I rarely hear one of them called in as Mighty Dead without the other. Victor and Cora Anderson are the founders of the Feri Tradition of Witchcraft, which emerged in the 1970s.

Victor Anderson's origin story is quite fantastical. He moved to Oregon as a young child, and early on met and was initiated by a Voodoo priest. As a young man he also trained to be a Kahuna, or Hawaiian priest. Prior to either of these experiences though, in 1926, Victor met a fairy woman in the woods of Oregon, who told him that she was a Feri Witch and so was he. Right in the moment of their meeting she initiated him. Throughout the 1930s he was involved with the Harpy Coven, a lineage coven of Witches located in Southern Oregon.

Cora Anderson grew up in Alabama. Her grandfather immigrated to the United States from Ireland and was a Druid. Locally, he became known as a root doctor, helping local people with the healing and magickal amelioration of spiritual, health, and magickal needs. He taught Cora much of the healing arts he practiced. Cora was well known for her psychic abilities and magickal work in the kitchen. Many have referred to Cora as the ultimate kitchen Witch.

In 1944, Victor and Cora met for the first time. They immediately felt connected and believed that they had met before on the astral plane. Three days after their first meeting they were married. In 1948, the Andersons moved to California and stayed there the rest of their lives. In the mid-1950s, Victor read *Witchcraft Today*, written by Gerald Gardner, and realized that the Witchcraft tradition they had been practicing was about to be put into the mainstream culture. It was at that point that they started creating working covens and teaching on a larger scale.

During the 1960s, the Andersons, mostly Victor, started to work with Gwyddion Pendderwyn, and the two of them crafted most of the practices and rituals that are still used in Feri today. Pendderwyn went on to initiate many other Witches in the line of Feri. There have been other prominent leaders in the Pagan and Witchcraft world that studied directly with Victor and Cora and then went off to start their own lines of the tradition.

It is well documented that Victor Anderson would teach a subject to one student one way and to another student a completely different, almost contradictory way. Practitioners of Feri don't seem to be bothered by these inconsistencies. And although many have refuted his origin stories, many others of the Feri lineage have expressed they have no reason to doubt any of his experiences.

Victor is believed to have created the practice of the Iron Pentacle, Pearl Pentacle, and brought the cleansing practice of the Kala rite into modern Paganism. The Feri Tradition is one of the largest and fastest growing traditions of modern Witchcraft. Whatever channeling or gifts that Victor, Cora, and Gwyddion may have had, they clearly have been worth holding on to. It is no surprise that the names of Victor Anderson and Cora Anderson are called as the Mighty Dead of the Craft; their voices are clearly folded into the tapestry of modern Witchcraft.

> *Anything worthwhile is dangerous.*
> —VICTOR ANDERSON,
> *EVOLUTIONARY WITCHCRAFT*

MARGOT ADLER (1946–2014)

Author, radio host, teacher, and priestess are just a few titles that could be given to Margot Adler. Her early life was rather uneventful, raised by her psychologist father in New York City. While attending UC Berkeley, Adler worked for KPFA radio station in the area. When she returned to New York in 1972, she created her own radio show, *Hour of the Wolf*. She worked as a journalist and reported through the radio station for most of her life.

In 1979, Margot Adler wrote one of the most important books for modern Witchcraft: *Drawing Down the Moon*. This book was written with a reporter's eye, using reporting-style language. The only difference between a detached reporter and Adler was the fact that Margot was an initiated Witch and was friends with many of the people she featured in her book.

Her book, and a book by Starhawk, *The Spiral Dance*, were published at the same time. Both are touted as the launch of feminist mainstream Wicca and Witchcraft. Adler's book should be read by anyone new to Witchcraft because it gives a clear picture of what the world of Paganism and Wicca was like in the 1970s. It was not easy in that time to find others practicing Witchcraft. Adler writes about her experience and shares the stories of many people who helped give birth to the modern Witchcraft movement.

Margot Adler was often described as "available," and this was true to the end of her life. She would often travel to Pagan events and festivals where she was known to give lectures and talks, and teach workshops. She was always very open and happy to speak with people. She was warm and inviting. If we give Gardner the credit for bringing Wicca into the public view, we can give Adler the credit of bringing it into the new age.

> *Magick is a convenient word for a whole collection*
> *of techniques, all of which involve the mind. In this*
> *case, we might conceive of these techniques as includ-*
> *ing the mobilization of confidence, will, and emotion*
> *brought about by the recognition of necessity; the use*
> *of imaginative faculties, particularly the ability to*
> *visualize, in order to begin to understand how*
> *other beings function in nature so we can use*
> *this knowledge to achieve necessary ends.*
> —MARGOT ADLER,
> DRAWING DOWN THE MOON

CONNECTING TO THE MIGHTY DEAD

Every tradition will have their own elders and leaders that may never be known outside of that lineage. Anyone that taught us anything about spirituality, Witchcraft, or Paganism was also, in turn, taught by someone themselves.

If all you've learned has been from books then you have the opportunity to discover the teachers of those authors who wrote the books that brought you along the path.

The first step in connecting to the Mighty Dead is to learn about them. Learn about those elders from your specific tradition that may have already crossed over. Go to your teachers and ask them about their teachers, and those that taught them, as far back as can be remembered. Modern Witchcraft lineage can be traced back rather easily. Learn the names of your own Mighty Dead and get pictures of them when possible.

Create a space in your home for the Mighty Dead. Ideally, this is a place separate from any other ancestor altar that you might already have. Samhain is always a good time to work with an ancestor altar, especially for the Mighty Dead, but if there is a specific time of the year that is more traditional or important in your lineage perhaps set up your Mighty Dead altar at that time.

Learn about the history of Witchcraft, Paganism, and Wicca. There is a lot of information out there and you don't have to know it all. At least acquaint yourself with some of the more common names, the more popular authors, and—more importantly—the names of those that inspired the popular modern authors.

Invite the Mighty Dead into your rituals. Call on them and name their names. When the Mighty Dead are invited in they can be asked for help or guidance. You can call on the Mighty Dead to help you gain skill or power in your Witchcraft practices. Find out what offerings they might desire (I've heard a good offering for Victor Anderson is Taco Bell) and make these offerings in trade for spiritual growth.

10

ALL THE DEAD

This section is filled with questions to ask yourself about your ancestry as well as practical things you can create to help you connect to your lineage. These items and questions are a jumping off point for you to begin to explore your relationship with your ancestors. Use the following formulas, tips, ideas, and questions while looking at your own ancestors, Mighty Dead, and Beloved Dead.

TAKING STOCK: ANCESTRAL EXERCISE

If this is your first foray into working with ancestors, it may be difficult to determine where to start. I encourage you to take stock of what you actually know about your lineage. Take some time to answer the following questions, giving time and thought to each one. Consider taking on these questions one by one. Ask your family or other Beloveds what their answers might be. Use these questions as a jumping off point to have deeper conversations. These questions can be explored with your ancestors, Beloved Dead, and

Mighty Dead. For ease, I am using the word *ancestors* to cover all of the dead throughout this section.

+ List your ancestors as far back as you can. Are you surprised by how much you do/don't know? Ask your loved ones if they can fill in any blanks.

+ What are some stories you know of your ancestors? Where did these stories come from? Did you witness any of these things or are they part of oral history?

+ Do you have any ancestral heirlooms? Where did these pieces come from? Why do you keep them? Do they have a financial value or is it all sentimental?

+ What are the cultural origins of your ancestors? How do you know this information? Have you done a DNA test? Can your loved ones fill in any blanks?

+ What are some ancestral traditions you still practice? What are the traditions that you keep? Where did these originate? How do you know this information?

A simple way to start the process of ancestor investigation is by talking to your living family members. Go through old photos with them and ask for names, dates, and stories that can be remembered. If they aren't already written down, write them down now. This is especially helpful to do on the backs of old family photos.

There are online resources that can help with this process as well. You can create an entire family tree using online services. This can help you to find names and lineage where your living family may be unable to help or remember.

Because this work can bring up painful information, difficult memories, or trauma, try to approach the work of it as an observer. It is easier to watch information unfold when you don't feel an emotional attachment to the outcome. This is easier said than done, but if you can keep a level of detachment it can also help you look with an observer's eye for patterns, synchronicity, or other information that you may not see if emotionally overwhelmed.

In the beginning, look at your most recent ancestors or names you know, and then start looking further back into the past. Where are the places your distant ancestors originated? Is it possible for you to go to these places?

Look at the threads and lineages of cultures that lead to you. How do you feel about these cultures? Are you proud to be descended from these places or do you feel concerned about them? How far back are you able to trace?

But don't stop there. Although it may not be possible to trace your ancestors back for a thousand years or more through a computer program, you can reach out to those ancestors through spiritual work. The names of our far past ancestors may have been lost, but they are still part of our makeup.

Time in the Otherworld doesn't flow like it does here in our realm. The far off ancestors may have had more time to understand the other side than your Beloved Dead have. They may be better equipped to help you even if you don't know their names at first.

Above all, remember this: just because you don't know someone as an ancestor doesn't mean they don't know you as a descendant.

CALLING THE DEAD

Before you do anything else with any of the ancestors, it is vital that you have an altar space where you can make them welcome. An ancestor altar doesn't have to be anything elaborate or expansive. A small and simple altar space works perfectly well. One of the most beautiful ancestor altars I've seen had a black and white framed photo, a white candle, and a glass of water.

ALTAR

Clear a space in your home for your ancestor altar. This could be the top of a bookshelf, a small side table, the corner of a desk, or a large tabletop. If you only have a small space and won't be able to have several altars, I highly recommend choosing an ancestor altar over any other option.

Start by cleansing the space. You will want to wipe down the space to clean it physically and spiritually. Furniture can hold the residue of previous uses. I get a lot of furniture from thrift stores and secondhand shops. We can't know the history of a piece of furniture. Before spiritual use, I always recommend a spiritual cleanse.

One way to cleanse an altar space is with a hyssop tea. Hyssop is an excellent herb for cleansing and protection. Make a tea with this herb and use the water to wash down your altar space. After you have washed it down, use an herbal smudge to further cleanse it. The smudge can be made with sage or cedar.

Next, put down an altar cloth. Ideally you should use fabric that came from an ancestor. This could be a scarf, a linen, or a piece of clothing. Anoint a large white candle with sandalwood oil and place it in the center of the altar space. Place a small drinking glass down next to the candle. If there was a favorite drink of your ancestors, pour this into the glass; otherwise, fill the glass with clear, fresh water.

Place as many pictures of your ancestors as you have and can fit in the space. This may require some creativity on your part to get them to fit. Or you may need to hang them up on the wall above the altar if there isn't enough room. If you possess any ashes, also place these on the altar space.

If you have any bowls or plates that belonged to your ancestors, place these on the altar space. If not, use a special bowl or plate where you can place offerings. Put a small fireproof bowl down next to the candle for incense burning.

Name your ancestors as you put this space together. Say any names that you know out loud. Also name any regions, countries, or places that were important to your ancestors. Name any and all ancestors that you plan to work with at this altar—blood, love, lineage, ancestors, Beloved Dead, and Mighty Dead. Light the candle and sit in meditation. When you feel complete, snuff out the candle.

Light the candle as often as you feel called to commune with your ancestors. Burn incense at these times too. Fill the glass and put offerings in the bowl on a daily basis.

ANCESTRAL HERBS AND MIXES

The following are herbs, minerals, and associations to help call in ancestral energy. Foods, drinks, or objects that specifically come from your ancestors, Beloved Dead, or Mighty Dead can also be added to the following list.

- Yew

- Apple

- Willow

- Elder

- Cypress

- Bean

- Lavender

- Sandalwood

- Linden

- Sage

- Black obsidian

+ Petrified wood

+ Bloodstone

ANCESTOR INCENSE #1

Use this incense blend on your ancestor altar when you want to actively call on your ancestors for help, guidance, or blessings.

1 part sage

1 part myrrh

1 part lavender

1 part linden

1 part sandalwood

ANCESTOR INCENSE #2

Use this incense blend any time you want to connect to your ancestors, but in a more passive way. This is not the incense to use when you want deep communion, rather when you want to passively send a thread of connection out.

1 part linden

1 part sandalwood

1 part lavender

1 part cedar

ANCESTOR WATER

This water is charged with ancestral bonds. It can be used as an offering to your ancestors, as a cleansing agent for an ancestor altar, and as an anointing liquid when stepping into ancestor work. Again, like with any of the ancestor mixes, add anything that would have held significance to your specific ancestors. It is best to make this water on a full moon so you can also utilize the moon energy to charge the mixture.

1 part water

1 part alcohol (vodka works perfectly)

1 bloodstone

1 pinch sandalwood

Put all of these ingredients together in a glass jar. As you put the ingredients together, pray over them. State out loud the names of your ancestors, Beloved Dead, and Mighty Dead that you know. Shake up the container and let it sit in your window sill on a full moon night. In the morning, strain the liquid, removing any of the sandalwood, but leaving in the bloodstone. Place it on your ancestor altar. I like to keep mine in a spray bottle so I can use it as needed on myself or other magickal objects connected to my ancestor working.

ANCESTRAL DIRT

In many traditions having the dirt from the gravesites of ancestors is a powerful way to work with your ancestors and bring some of their energy into your home. Getting graveyard dirt is simple enough if your ancestors are buried in a place that is easily accessible. If you are lucky enough to have access to your ancestors' graves, collect the dirt, but only after leaving them an offering or "paying" for the dirt.

It is customary in many traditions—especially Afro-Caribbean traditions—to pay for graveyard dirt. This is done by first asking permission to take the dirt, and when you feel the request has been granted, putting a coin on the headstone and taking some of the soil from the gravesite.

There are many reasons that graveyard dirt might not be available. It could be that there isn't a grave for your ancestor, or they were buried too far away. Perhaps your ancestors were cremated or there is some other reason. There are other types of dirt that can also work.

Try to collect dirt from a family home, near a city square where your ancestors once lived, or some other important location to your family or lineage. At the very least collect dirt from the village, city, or town where your ancestors lived. Mix all your ancestral dirt together and keep it in a glass jar; this is a representation of you and the mixture that you are. Keep this jar on your altar.

FORGOTTEN DEAD

It would not be possible to talk of the ancestors without spending a moment on the forgotten dead. Millions of people have died that no one remembers. Millions. There are more forgotten dead than remembered dead. Giving a nod to those that have been forgotten feeds the deep ancestral well that we are all connected to.

There are also the forgotten dead of the Craft. The Witches, teachers, midwives, herbalists, wortcunners, root doctors, and priestesses that hid their practices in the dark. Those Witches that were brave enough to teach what they knew to at least one other person. There are those Mighty Dead that did the work of lineage building and torch bearing when no one knew what they were doing.

It is to these forgotten dead that we owe more than we can ever fully comprehend. It is to these dead that we owe gratitude and love, those whose names are gone and whose lineages have been lost to the sands of time. We mourn them in order to avoid losing any more.

Section Three

CONNECTION

11

WORKING WITH THE FAE

One of the biggest issues that modern people face is a disconnection from the Land. I think this is a serious problem, and a major source of unease. Many modern Witches and Pagans are working to reconnect with these relationships, but the loss of connection to the Land and the Spirits of the Land is a major factor in why we (as a culture) are allowing so many environmental atrocities to take place. If our society and culture was connected to our Land and aware that we are not alone, are inter-connected, need each other, and need the Land, we would be in a much better place.

I am capitalizing Land here to convey a deeper meaning and power behind the word. This isn't just the dirt in your backyard or the hills or landscape. The Land is a living, breathing force. The Land holds an energy and is filled with spirits.

Disconnection and disillusionment is an illness of modern culture. We hold this idea that we are alone, that we have to pick ourselves up by our bootstraps, and that we have to get it done all on our own. When we can't even depend on each other, how can we be expected to feel connected to the Land around us?

We are also told/taught/shown that the Land is a series of resources. The Land gives us our food, our oil, our metals, and gemstones. We build our homes on the Land. The Land is a thing that we use. It gives to us, but how often are we giving back? As a Witch or a Pagan you may have one answer, but what about the average person? How often do they see their connection to the Land around them?

Those of us that are non-Native to the Land we live on have an additional problem of living on land that was stolen from Native peoples. How do we walk the balance of honoring the Land (as an entity), while acknowledging that it was stolen? And how do we do that without culturally appropriating the Native cultures that are still connected to the landscape? This is a tricky place to be. However, it is vital and important work—probably the most important work that we can do as modern Witches and Pagans.

The access to travel (cars, planes, trains) has also changed how we relate to a place. It is so easy to get from one place to another. People move with much more frequency than they did in the past. We don't have the deep connection to Land like our ancestors did. This is true for most modern peoples, but as an American, I feel that it is even more of an American issue, almost an illness if you will. An illness of disconnection.

As a teenager in the mid-1990s, I had access to a car and I grew up in a suburban environment. But I also walked everywhere in my little town. I knew all the back roads and how to get to my friend's houses without being seen on the main streets. I knew how to sneak around the park to avoid being seen by other kids. I knew the secret hiding places (or as we called them, "clubhouses") along the golf course. I knew where there were bushes large enough to hide six kids in our apartment complex. I knew the places where I felt an uncomfortable stirring in my gut or where the hairs on my arms would stand on end, and I would avoid those places. I knew the natural hidden places where it was safe and cozy, and where even in the rain the bushes were thick enough to keep me dry.

At the age of ten I didn't think of my relationship to the Spirits of the Land, but I definitely had one. When I go back into those neighborhoods of my childhood, I can still feel those threads of connection and the energy of those Spirits. It's like seeing an old friend after many years away. A little awkward at first, but still comfortable.

Modern Pagans and Witches will not be able to work with the Land as the ancestors of this Land did. We have to find other ways, new ways, modern ways of honoring the Land Spirits and being in personal relationship with them. We say *what is remembered lives*, and there are no other beings that need to be honored and remembered more than the Spirits of the Land, which I also refer to as the Fae.

Fae beings are not one type of being. When I use the term *Fae* I am describing a whole class of beings that have hundreds (if not more) subtypes, species, and genuses. Beings from different parts of the world may be called different names, but are related. Beings from different parts of the world may seem similar, but are totally unique and unrelated. The scientific classification of the Fae is a very complicated flow chart. We humans don't fully understand it and we can't fully chart it either.

When someone says Seelie Court, the Good People, or the Shining Ones, they are usually referring to the Fae beings that are more willing to be in relationship with humans, the "nice ones." On the other hand, when people refer to the Unseelie Court, the Dark Fae, or the Dangerous Ones, they are typically referring to the Fae beings to watch out for. The idea is that these Fae beings may mean to harm us; they are dangerous, malicious, or cruel.

The concept of Seelie and Unseelie Courts is a British construct that is based on the Victorian obsession with fairies. The hierarchy that exists in these court systems is descended from the hierarchy of the British monarchy and has no real bearing on how the Fae orient themselves. *Seelie* and *Unseelie* are pretty words that we humans use to try to describe what we are not capable of understanding.

Often there is an assumption of the Fae being Celtic or European in origin, but most cultures on earth have Fae beings of some kind, they just might not be called *fairies*. There are many places in the world where the Fae are still honored and revered. Ireland, Iceland, Japan, Hawaii, South Africa, and more all have active Fae beliefs. In most cases, these cultures never fully lost their connection to the Land around them and the spirits that inhabit their landscape. When we (humans) are connected to the Land, we tend to honor the Fae.

As we move forward in this section I will use the word *Fae* interchangeably with *Land Spirit*, *Spirit of Place*, and *Spirit of the Land*. These beings include the Sidhe of the Celtic people, the Elves of the Norse, the Banshee of the Irish, the Menehune from Hawaii, Abatwa of South Africa, and even Angels from the Abrahamic faiths. All of these spirits are types of Fae.

When I talk about the Fae, I am using that term to describe Nature Spirits in all their forms. There will not be a large focus on the specific tribes of Fae beings or the cultural Fae beings from different parts of the world. As you read on you won't find an encyclopedia of different phylum of Fae. Rather, the focus will be on *connecting* to the Nature Spirits of *your* Land and your local environment.

The best place to start a relationship with the Fae is in your own home. It doesn't matter if you live in a studio apartment or on an expansive parcel of land, there are Fae all around you. There is no better time to start connecting to the Fae than right now.

One of the things that often comes up with connecting with the Fae is the question of "realness." How do we know when an experience is real? How do we know when we have had an encounter? Experiences with Otherworldly beings aren't always rational, clear, or obvious. Sometimes encounters are subtle or only seen with a sideways glance. An experience with the Otherworld will often be unexpected. You may find yourself unable to explain something that has happened or it may feel so odd or unusual that you can't easily brush it off.

With any type of Otherworld encounter there may be a desire to find a rational explanation. I refer to this as rationalizing the mystical away.

It's human nature to look for a logical explanation rather than a magickal or mystical one, especially from a modern perspective. A mystical experience can be scary, weird, or unsettling. Not having a clear reason for something happening can leave us feeling shaken or surprised. We might have to admit that there are things in this world that we can't see (or can't see in the way we see the rest of the world). We may have to face the fact that we have less control over our environments than we previously believed. We may have to come to terms with the fact that we are not alone.

When you start opening up to the Fae realms, you may find some of the following things start to happen:

- Loss of an item that you always keep in the same place, only to have it reappear in the exact same place later.

- Loss of an item that reappears later in a place where you would never have put it.

- Loss of an item that you regularly use and never find again, even if it would be impossible for you to have moved it.

- Seeing movement out of the corner of your eye, but seeing nothing there when you look directly at it.

- Seeing beings out of the corner of your eye that are clearly not of this world.

- Seeing beings clearly that are not of this world.

- Hearing noises in your home that have no rational explanation— beyond the house "settling."

- Finding trinkets that seem to have been left for you. This could be things like little bones, feathers, leaves, sparkly bits, or buttons.

- Hearing/seeing/feeling/receiving messages when you are in the places where you do your work with the Fae.

Opening up to the spirits of your place, the Fae beings where you live, brings you into a greater harmony with your environment. It brings a better depth and understanding to the cycles that happen right where you live.

I've lived in the same town for a really long time. And I've been in the same house for over a decade. I know that right around Imbolc the daffodils sprout. I know that right around Lammas the naked ladies sprout (often in the same places the daffodils were earlier in the year). In years of drought, the big tree in the backyard loses its leaves later in the year. In years when we've have flooding, the big tree loses its leaves earlier.

The robin shows up in the early days of spring. The barn owl shares a hunting ground with the red shouldered hawk. Once or twice a year the crows gather for some sort of raucous council that lasts about an hour. Rarely do I see a raccoon, but I often get a whiff of skunk. A gobble of turkeys comes in and out of the yard, roosting in the tree in the late fall.

I know my place. I am in tune with its cycles and seasons. I respect the plants and animals that live here with me. And because of this awareness, living with—and in—these cycles, I know when things are off. I know when there is trouble. I know when I need to be cautious or leave out extra food or water for the wild ones.

When looking to connect with the Spirits of your Land, or the Fae where you live, you are also dealing with different types of Fae and how they might relate to you. There may be a small Nature Spirit or house spirit that only takes up a tiny amount of space. But you may also find yourself encountering a tree spirit, the spirit of a hillside, copse of trees, vineyard, or mountain. There are small beings that could fit on the top of a pinhead, larger spirits that fill an entire county, and amorphous spirits that have no shape or form and can show up in a myriad of ways.

It is easy to think small when we think Fae, and a lot of that has to do with the information we get from the over-culture. We think of fairies as sweet, small, winged creatures. These beings do exist, but there are also smaller and much much larger beings too. You may encounter the spirit of a specific oak tree or the spirit of all oak trees. Allow each potential connection to unfold as something unique and special.

THE STORY OF YOUR LAND

Do you know how your home came to be? I mean both your actual dwelling *and* the town it resides in. Do you know when your town or city was settled and by whom? Do you know the name of the peoples that lived in that area before settlers arrived? Are you aware of any battles that may have happened near you?

Learn the history of your Land as a way of knowing its story. The Land itself will have a story to tell, but this will only be one piece, one picture. Take some time to explore the human history of your Land. This will fill in the blanks that the Spirits of the Land may not be able to fully convey. It may be difficult to learn the history of your Land. Many places have sad, terrible, and ugly stories of war, death, and colonization. But you need to know. Blood spilt on the Land leaves a powerful marker. Understanding that marker can help you to offer healing and reparations where needed.

Most small towns have a hall of records or even museums where intricate and small details are saved. You might not be able to find this information online. Especially in the Western United States, where some states aren't even two hundred years old, these histories are kept only by small local museums and historians.

In my little town there are still elders who remember the incorporation, who were here when this rural land was sold to developers. The history of the handful of white men that shaped this town and several towns around it is easy to learn. But there are smaller stories, bits of history, sad tales, and shocking violence that are kept only in the local museums. And these stories are eager to be told, shared, and remembered.

LOCAL FLORA AND FAUNA

There is much to glean about the Spirits of the Land from the plants and animals that live around your area. Fae are comfortable with the other Nature Spirits that live in our world, like plants and animals. Fae are likely to hang out in gardens and other places where there may be more natural activity.

Although working with plant and animal spirits is different than the Fae, there are some similarities. If you live near a vineyard, you are more likely to encounter Fae beings that are familiar with grapes, cultivation, and the plants and animals that make their homes in vineyards. It will be helpful in developing your relationships to study the energies of these creatures too.

This is also true when you work with, or connect with, a specific plant. For a period of time, milk thistle starting growing in my yard after I had been living in the same place for five years with no milk thistle. It's not an easy plant to get rid of, and after a few attempts at eradication I decided to look up the plant.

Its healing properties were in direct alignment with what was going on in my life at that time. It was an ally that I needed. When I started to reach out to the plant being and develop a relationship with the green blood, I also encountered a Fae being that was connected to this plant.

Interactions with Fae beings are often difficult to put into words. And as a very rational and skeptical person I have struggled with some of my Fae interactions because they are often so weird. But when I started to connect to milk thistle as a plant, I was introduced to Milk Thistle as a Nature Spirit that has become a Fae ally of mine. (Milk Thistle is not the actual name of this ally. That would be too Disney perfect. But it is as close as I can get with limited language.) The only way that I can describe this Spirit is like watching a small glowing being that enters, or incorporates with, the plant, helping it to grow and fostering its healing abilities. The plant and the Fae being have a collaborative relationship.

It was by being shown the intricacies of their relationship that I was able to better understand the need of milk thistle in my own life. And when Milk Thistle shows up, I understand completely the message and what I need to do.

It is also through this relationship that I was shown the intricacies of other plant, animal, Fae, and human relationships in the biosphere. Through Milk Thistle I was shown the vast web of Fae beings that interact with plant life on the micro and the macro. The ecosystem of plant life that we are really only beginning to understand is spiritually made a bit more complicated due to the layer of Fae interaction that weaves into it.

FAE COURTESIES

The rules in the Fae realm are different than they are here. What you might not see as a slight could be considered very rude in the Fae realms. It is important when working with these beings that you not offend them or treat them poorly. This is where people get into trouble with the Fae. They don't have the same temperament as humans, so don't expect human reactions.

More often than not, I find the Fae beings to be rather impatient with my human foibles. Sometimes it can feel like the Fae is a strict adult nanny and I am a toddler. I don't really understand the rules, I'm kind of bumbling around, and they have very little patience for my fumbling in their realms.

IRON

Iron is considered a no-no for working with the Fae realms. However, this likely comes from Roman superstition from when they were first invading the British Isles. The Romans were afraid of the magick that the Britons and Celts possessed. The Celts adorned themselves in woad and white chalk and it was believed that they could disappear into the forest or even the clouds. The Britons' weapons were made from bronze, the Romans' from iron. Therefore, the belief came about that iron could fight off the Fae beings, actually meaning the Roman weapons could destroy the Celts.

However, this superstition has survived for a reason. So much so that immigrants from the British Isles and Ireland brought these tales to the United States. That is no easy feat for any folktale.

Iron is also a grounding metal. It is used in lightning rods to draw off the charge and ground it into the earth. Many magickal systems suggest not working with iron or even having anything made of iron in magickal circles. Humans have high iron content in our bodies, which also shows our relationship to the earth, to grounding, to "this realm." All of these things could add to the belief of the Fae not liking iron.

In my experience there are many types of Fae beings that find iron offensive, yes. But it is also true that many Fae beings don't care for manmade items or weapons at all. I have not found that iron is destructive to the Fae, but for the most part they don't care for it. However, up to this point in my practice I've never had a lump of raw iron to offer a Fae being. Maybe someday.

SPEAKING TO THEM

There are levels and layers of courtesies that may seem odd to a modern practitioner, especially an American one. Sadly, we Americans tend to be a little too brash at times and this is highly off-putting to most Fae beings. It is considered rude to speak of the Fae as if they aren't present—because they always are. The same is true when speaking about another human in the room with you as if they weren't there.

It is considered bad form to call them fairies or Fae directly. This is why, especially in Ireland and Iceland—two places where working with the Fae is still very much a thriving practice—they have plenty of other names for the Fae beings. It's almost like you have to approach them from the side, with a sidelong glance, or looking out of the corner of your eye, even when you are only talking about them.

SECRETS

In the workshops I teach on Witchcraft and Paganism, I ask my students to keep a level of confidentiality for what we do in class. Personally, I'm an open book and I don't mind folks sharing things I say or do, but there may be students that are not "out of the broom closet" and it goes back to old school Witchcraft rules to keep silent about other students, what they share, and their experiences.

This is also true when it comes to the Spirits of Place. If you get a message or have an interaction, be cautious who you share that experience with. If given the opportunity, always ask the Spirits of Place if they are willing for you to share what they have told or given you. This is just good manners.

More often than not, they are happy for you to share, but sometimes information is just for you. You will gain more favor being polite than making assumptions (which is really a good rule of thumb all the time).

FAE LAND

Be respectful of their places and dwellings. There are stories from all over the world of Fae dwellings or meeting places being destroyed, often for modern convenience and progress. These places tend to be fraught with complications, delays, accidents, and other troublesome issues. When you become familiar with Fae places, work to keep them safe and unharmed.

KEEP YOUR WORD

It is important that you keep your word with Fae beings and Spirits of the Land. If you say that you are going to do something. you'd better do it. Show up when you say you are going to show up. Give them what you say you are going to give them. And be very cautious of making any kind of deals, trades, or bargains with them. All is not what it seems and they are very good at making deals that benefit them more than it might seem on the surface.

OFFERINGS

Once you start a relationship with a Fae, be prepared to keep it going. If you start to leave offerings every full moon and then you suddenly stop, you might find you have an irritated Fae being on your hands. This is especially true if you are only leaving offerings and not really working to develop a deeper relationship. I find that people who dabble with Fae relationships tend to have more mischief pop up in their homes and in their lives.

WHERE IS THE FAE REALM?

Remember the idea of the cosmic croissant? A croissant has layers and layers of tangible pastry and lots of air, bubbles, and space. One of these layers of the cosmic croissant is the Fae realms. They are right next to and intermixed with our realms. There are doors and portals into the Fae realms, but they should not ever be entered without a Fae guide. The realm of the Spirits of the Land does not function like the human realm. Entering without proper preparation could lead to illness, madness, or worse.

Until you have forged a solid relationship with a Fae being, don't go wandering around in their realms. It is not a good idea to go into neighborhoods that you are unfamiliar with. Even the Fae that have the patience to help you out might just leave you to it to teach you a lesson. It is notoriously hard to find your way out of the Fae realms once you've gone in. Unlike the astral realms you may be used to traveling in, the roads that you follow into the Fae realms may not lead back out. Nothing is what it seems.

CREATE SPACE

The best way to open up a relationship with the Fae is to make space for them and let them know the space is for them. This may sound simple enough, but making the determination of where to place their space can be rather tricky. Making space for the Fae, or Spirits of the Land, around you requires paying attention and noticing where there may already be places that you haven't been paying attention to. It requires trusting your intuition and instincts on where the Spirits are in your home and surrounding areas.

It is likely that there are already Fae living in and around your home. They don't need to be invited in, they don't need your acknowledgment, and you may or may not already recognize that they are there. Connecting to the Spirits of the Land where you live is really about noticing where these beings already are and taking time to welcome them, letting them know that you acknowledge their existence and want to develop a relationship with them.

The first step in this process is actually really simple. Just sit. Sit in your space with an open heart, mind, and spirit. You can do this in every room of your home, in your front yard, backyard, patio, balcony, garage, or any place where you might be curious or interested in discovering where the Fae may already be. The following exercise can be done in any space of your home, inside or outside. The process is written for a small backyard, but it can be adjusted to work in any place. It can also be used for local parks, camping sites, favorite outdoor spots, picnic sites, and so much more.

FINDING THE FAE IN YOUR SPACE

Go out into your yard and find a place where you can sit undisturbed for at least twenty minutes. You will need to return to this place every day for a least a week, but ideally this is a place where you should return often throughout the year and at different times of the day. This isn't a meditation or a journey; this is a sit spot.

People who do tracking or hunting are likely familiar with the concept of a sit spot. When you return to the same place in your yard over and over again, you become familiar with that place. You begin to see patterns. You begin to tune into the landscape and flora and fauna that live there. It's important that while you are in your sit spot you blend into the space. Not like camouflage, but a blending in, a becoming part of the space. The point is to connect to the Land and the Spirits that dwell there. To remember that you are connected to this Land and the Spirits. You don't want to come in stomping around with poor manners like a rude tourist. You want to immerse yourself in the landscape and fold yourself into what is already happening.

When you are in your spot, just sit, but also pay attention, especially to your peripheral vision. Be in your place and watch what happens. Be present. Notice what you see out of the corner of your eyes. Notice places where something may be off, odd, or different. Take note of any places where there is too much of something or, conversely, not enough. Any areas where Fae are already spending time will start to stand out to you.

Fae spots may also be present in naturally occurring spots—holes in a tree, rock formations, interesting or odd bends in plant life, old trees, naturally occurring crossroads (and occasionally man-made crossroads too), places where plant life seems to be circular, mushroom rings, and other interesting places. Watch these places, but don't try to go into them!

This may not become obvious the first time you go to your sit spot. It may take several days or even weeks before it becomes clear, but you are working on developing a relationship with the Fae, and relationships take time. You need to show the Spirits of the Land that you are trustworthy.

Once you locate the spaces where the Fae are spending time, you can create shrines, altars, or offering spots for them. These spaces can have things as simple as a plant, a stack of stones, an offering bowl, or even one of those little fairy houses. It helps to know what kind of spirit you are working with, but this may not be discernible at first.

My favorite thing to do is to create a little dolmen of stones. Dolmens are megalithic chambers made out of stones, which are found across Europe, the UK, and Ireland. Often thought to be burial chambers, these stone structures have been discovered in many parts of the world and we still don't really know why.

I was taught that dolmens are portals. They are doorways that can help us connect to the unseen realms, including the Fae realms and the ancestral realms. Creating a large megalithic-style dolmen in your backyard may not be a possibility, but you can create a smaller version of this same concept.

By making a small stack of stones, a little archway, or even a little structure, you create a place where you can show the Fae that they are welcome. When creating this place for them, make sure you explain what you are doing. Let them know this is a place you are making specifically for them. Let them know that they are welcome.

This may require you to speak to invisible beings in your backyard. Yes, this may mean looking a little odd. Not everyone in your life is going to "get" it. People may find the concept of speaking to Spirits of the Land in your backyard totally ridiculous (even other Witches and Pagans). Yes, it is a little odd, but developing relationship with these beings is fulfilling. And in my opinion, if we are going to live in shared space with them anyway, it's just good manners to let them feel welcome.

FAE ATTRACTANTS

The following items are known to attract the Fae. There are also recipes for specific blends that I have used to help call the Fae. They can be worn (assuming you have checked for allergic reaction), used as offerings, or used during ritual when you may want to call the Fae to your circle. I have also included Fae tea recipes. Having tea with the Spirits of the Land is an excellent way to connect with them. Discovering the plants that naturally grow in your land and adjusting any tea recipes to add these in works to connect more deeply to your land.

HERBS TO DRAW THE FAE

+ Primrose

+ Rosemary

+ Straw

+ Thyme

+ Clover

+ Rosehips

+ Damiana

+ Thistle

FLOWERS TO DRAW THE FAE

+ Gardenia

+ Liliac

+ Tuberose

+ Dandelion

- Magnolia
- Violet
- Lavender

HERBS TO PROTECT FROM THE FAE

- Gorse
- Peony

TREES TO DRAW THE FAE

There is a long-held superstition that a mixture of oak, ash, and thorn can be used to call in the Fae. This is a Victorian-era belief, but it likely has older folk origins. Any place where the oak, ash, and thorn trees grow together is a natural place for the Fae to gather. These trees don't naturally occur in all areas of the world. Look at the trees that grow in your area and see if there are places where they grow together. These are likely to be places of magickal confluence. These are great places to start looking for Fae.

- Oak
- Ash
- Hawthorne
- White thorn

FAE INCENSE BLEND #1

1 part thyme

1 part rosemary

1 part straw

Use a mortar and pestle to ground the herbs into small pieces, then burn on a charcoal any time you want to call the Fae into a ritual.

FAE INCENSE BLEND #2

1 part thyme

1 part damiana

1 part lavender

10 drops lilac oil

Use a mortar and pestle to ground the herbs into a powder. Put the drops of oil on the powder and mix until fully incorporated. Burn the mixture on a charcoal any time you want to call the Fae into a ritual.

FAE INCENSE BLEND #3

1 part lavender

1 part clover

1 part violet

10 drops magnolia oil

10 drops tuberose oil

Use a mortar and pestle to ground the herbs into a powder. Add the drops of oil on the powder and mix until fully incorporated. Burn the mixture on a charcoal any time you want to call the Fae into a ritual.

FAERIE TEA #1

3 parts black tea

1 part chamomile

1 part dandelion root

1 part elderberry

1 part hops

1 part mullein

1 part raspberry leaf

1 part rose hips

FAERIE TEA #2

1 part chamomile

1 part thyme

1 part yarrow

1 part rose hips

1 part mugwort

FAE CHARM BAG

Create this charm bag to help you connect to the Spirits of the Land. The ingredients are generic so that this working can be done in any part of the world, but for this charm bag to be the most effective, add herbs that grow naturally in your area. You can either wear this charm bag on your person when you are doing specific work with the Fae or you can leave it in the areas were the Fae reside around your home.

This work is best done during the months of May or November, when the doors to the Fae realms are the most open. This ritual is written for a group, but can be easily modified for a solitary practitioner. You will need to pick one of your group to represent the High Priestess for this ritual, and their lines will be noted below as spoken by "HP."

SUPPLIES

one green square of fabric for each participant

sewing supplies

stones and/or crystals

dandelion

lavender

damiana

bowl of soil

bowl of water

cedar incense

white candle

RITUAL

Go to a place where there is strong Fae activity. This may be the Fae spot of one of the people in your circle. If you don't yet have one, complete this ritual at an outdoor location. One of the ritualists will need to light the incense and the candle. Each participant will sew up all of the items into their fabric, creating a small pillow.

HP says:

> We call upon the elements to charge and awaken this
> charm that it may call the Spirits of the Land to us.
> We call upon the elements to bless and consecrate this
> charm, so it will aid us in our work with the Fae.

With each of the following steps, the HP will state a line and the participants will repeat it.

Each participant sprinkles their charm bag with the soil. The HP says:

By the Earth, may this charm be solid.
(Participants repeat)

Each participant runs their bag through the smoke of the incense. The HP says:

By the Air, may this charm open communication.
(Participants repeat)

Each participant passes their bag through the flame. The HP says:

By the Fire, may this charm bring connection.
(Participants repeat)

Each participant sprinkles the charm bag with water. The HP says:

By the Water, may this charm bring relationship.
(Participants repeat)

HP says:

We consecrate these charms by the power
of the elements. So mote it be!
(Participants repeat)

Each participant should further charge their bags by breathing on them. This will wake them up and give them life. When each person feels complete and is done, the HP says:

This charm is blessed for our work
with the Fae. So mote it be!
(Participants repeat)

You can now wear this charm when you want to communicate with your Fae allies or keep it in a place where you work with them.

WELCOME FAE RITUAL

Once you have established a connection with Spirits of the Land in or around your home, do a ritual to mark that relationship. This is a way to show the Fae that you are committed to an ongoing relationship with them.

This ritual is written for a solitary practitioner, but can be easily modified for a group or coven.

SUPPLIES

handful of small stones

incense mix from the list on page 198 and 199

fresh flowers

sweet cakes

wand

offerings

blanket

SET UP

This ritual should be done in the place where you have located Fae activity. You will need a handful of stones, ideally stones that are slightly smaller than your palm. Choose one of the incense mixes from the list of Fae attractants. Have some fresh flowers, ideally flowers from the Fae attractant list or locally-grown flowers. You will also need sweet cakes, your wand, and a small personal offering that you will be giving them. If you aren't sure what offering to leave, read the section on offerings on page 214. If you are heading to a spot outdoors, take a blanket or something comfortable for you to sit on while you do this ritual.

RITUAL

Lay out your ritual items in and around the area where you have detected Fae activity. Lay out your blanket and create a comfortable place for yourself. Lay out your wand, the stones, flowers, cakes, and incense. Place everything on the ground.

Take a moment to ground and center yourself, bringing your awareness into full presence. Before you cast your circle, take a moment to look around this place. Look with your eyes, your third eye, your heart. Note any Fae activity happening in the moment. Just notice how it feels and what is going on in the present.

Pick up your wand and cast your circle, including the Fae space in your circle. Face the area where you have been working with the the Fae and say this:

> Welcome to the Spirits of this Place. Welcome to the
> Fae. I call upon you to join me in this ritual. I call
> upon you as an ally. I call upon you as a guardian of
> this place. I honor you, Spirits.

Sit down and allow yourself to be comfortable. Sink back into that place of groundedness and focus. Breathe and be present. Sit in this place for as long as you feel called. Notice any Fae activity that may happen while you are there. Since this is a place where you have already started to connect to the Spirits of the Land, allow a conversation with this place to unfold.

When you feel complete, use the stones to create a dolmen. A dolmen can be a small stone structure or a simple stack. As you create this structure, speak out loud, sharing with the Spirits what it is you are doing. Let them know that you are creating this place for them, as a magickal dwelling.

Put your offering right in front of the dolmen. Again, speak out loud to let the Spirits of this Place know that this offering is for them. Speak from your heart, sharing why this is a special object and why you are gifting this offering to them. Place some of the sweet cake down near the dolmen and speak out loud that this is an offering for the beings of this place. Eat some of this sweet cake yourself, but not from the piece that you set down as an offering.

When you feel ready, begin the process to end your ritual. Say this:

> *I am grateful to you, Spirits of this Place. I am*
> *grateful to you, Fae. Thank you for joining me in*
> *this ritual. I honor you as my ally. I honor you as a*
> *guardian of this place. I honor you, Spirits. Thank*
> *you. From this circle, I bid you hail and farewell.*

Lay the flowers out around the area, clean up your ritual space, and use your wand to open the circle that you created. Leave the dolmen and offerings for the Fae. If this is a wild place, your offerings must be natural. Take anything else with you, including garbage that was left by other people that you find on your way back.

• ——◆·◆·◆—— •

FINDING THE FAE IN OTHER PLACES

• ——◆·◆·◆—— •

You may also want to try to connect with the Fae beings that live in and around your home environment or further afield. Connecting with the Spirits of the Land out in the wild is just a little bit different than connecting to the Spirits in and around your home.

The Fae "in the wild" may have even less of a concept of interacting with humans than Fae that may already live in your house. You are much more likely to run into larger beings, stranger beings, and beings that are frightening. But just like the beauty that you can experience in the wilds of nature, the Fae that are in the wild places contain a beauty that is found nowhere else.

A sit spot is still the best practice for locating Fae out in the wilds, but there is also more to consider. Like I said before, the concept of a sit spot is something that hunters and trackers use all of the time. When out in the wilds of nature there are other things to know about finding the perfect sit spot that also translates quite well to a sit spot for Fae beings and other Land Spirits. Here are some things to consider when seeking out a wild sit spot.

- Consider a place where there is running water. Running water brings access to lots of different types of Spirits, including those that live *in* the water. It can also work to bring more wild into your home sit spot by putting in a small water feature or fountain.

- Find a liminal space. Liminal spaces are the between places. The beach is a perfect example of a liminal space. The beach is land, but it is also sea; it is wet, but it is also dry. The edge of a forest, the edge of a grassland, a tree line that separates this field from that vineyard—these are all liminal spaces. Land

Spirits are often drawn to the edges, the liminal spots. These are natural magickal places.

+ Keep yourself blended in as part of the landscape. Just like you do when you are in your sit spot at your own home, blend in as much as possible. This isn't like hunting, when you need to blend in and not be seen; it is highly unlikely that you will go unseen. But when you show that you are putting forth the effort to be a part of the energy of the Land around you, the Fae are more likely to interact with you or connect with you.

+ Pay attention to your surroundings. Just like you pay attention in your own home or yard, watch what is going on in this sit spot area. This means two things. First, watch the plants and animals that are moving about and living in this area. What do you notice about these creatures? Are there any specific plants or animals that you feel a connection with? These can also be significators of Fae beings. The second thing is to watch the shapes, shadows, and movements that take place in the corners of your sight. What is going on just over there? What was that shimmer? What was that shadow? Not everything is going to be Fae movement, but some of it could be. The more tuned in you are, the more likely you are to notice when they make subtle movements around you.

THE WILD HUNT

The Wild Hunt comes from European folklore, and threads of the story are found over almost all of Europe. In the tales, ghostly, phantom, or Fae beings ride through a town or village in the middle of the night. Often the Wild Hunt would come through on a night when there was strong wind or dangerous weather.

If any humans were out and about during the Wild Hunt, they would be caught up in the charge and would find themselves miles from home afterward. There were also superstitions that during the Wild Hunt anyone sick or weak may also be carried off by the hunters, and it is still common for folks in Northern Europe to close their windows when someone in the house is ill.

Modern Witches and Pagans have taken the Wild Hunt in an additional and, some might argue, more old-school direction. The Wild Hunt has been enacted in many Pagan rituals as a way of bringing out the wild, breaking tight restrictions, and allowing human participants to reconnect to the wild that is often a forgotten part of being human.

The following exercise is a trance that should be done in your Place of Power to allow for maximum safety. If doing this in a group, have someone lead the trance. If doing this solo, record it beforehand. Start with the trance induction.

TRANCE

Open your inner eye and see before you the door that leads to your Place of Power. Knock three times on the door, turn the handle, and step through into the center of your Place of Power. Take a moment to look around, noting anything that stands out or is interesting at this moment. Breathe in, listen, and look for a path that will lead you to where the Wild Hunt is taking place.

Walk to this path and allow your feet to carry you forward. Step by step you move down the path, and as you do the sky around you begins to darken and the wind picks up. The path continues and you keep moving forward, one foot in front of the other. (Pause)

You come to a clearing, an open space, where there is a break in the clouds and the moon shines through. You step into this clearing and the wind picks up even more, whipping around you. In the distance you hear the galloping of horses' hooves and the shouting of voices. The wind carries with it the sounds of revelry and it seems as if these noises are swirling through this clearing. There is a scent on the wind, a scent of wild spaces, sweaty bodies, and lightning.

The Wild Hunt peeks through, breaking into the clearing. There are dozens, hundreds, thousands, an untold number of Fae beings. Some are on horseback, some are on their feet, and some are flying on their own wings. They are whooping and hollering. They are celebrating, singing, and making a major ruckus.

The revelers swing around the edges of the clearing, coming closer and closer to you. Their noise and music get more deafening. You find yourself feeling called to the party. The sound of the music fills your bones and awakens your blood. Your body begins to move to the sounds, and as the Hunt reaches you, you find yourself easily and happily carried along.

The Wild Hunt moves back out of the clearing, picking up speed, noise, and frenzy. You move with them, easily a part of the pack now. You whoop and holler. You sing and dance. The Fae around you include you in their revels. (Pause) You continue to travel along with the Wild Hunt, feel the wildness move through you, and let yourself go into that energy. (Pause)

The Hunt continues and you move along with it. Suddenly you see the clearing where the revels began. The Wild Hunt carries you through into the clearing, moving again in a circle, coming ever closer and closer to the center. As you reach the center, the Hunt moves on without you, leaving you alone. The wind, song, and flurry of bodies flows around you and away. The sound of revelry moves back out of the clearing, the scent of wild on the air begins to dissipate, and you find the pulse of the music slowly leaving you as the Hunt moves further and further away.

You begin to feel a sense of calm and centeredness. As you look around the clearing, you see a gift left behind by the Wild Hunt. Pick up this gift and examine it. Take a moment to look at this gift and see what information comes through. Place this gift in a place where you can hold onto it. Your feet take you back to the path that brought you to this place. Step by step you move back through this place to the center of your Place of Power. One foot in front of the other, you walk along the path leading you back out.

When you reach the center of your Place of Power, you move to the door, carrying your gift from the Fae along with you. Close the door behind you and close your inner eye. Let your Witch's eye close, and as it does, notice your physical body.

Allow yourself to feel your skin and your breathing. Let yourself become fully present in your body. Slowly open your eyes and pat your edges. Say your name out loud three times.

Take a moment to write down this experience. Welcome back!

If you can, immediately go outside for a walk and see if the gift you received manifests in the physical world. Pay attention over the next few days and weeks for this gift to show up in other places too.

OTHERWORLD ALLY QUEST

You may find that you have many Fae allies and companions in this world, but you can also gain Fae allies and companions by visiting the Otherworld through the portal that is your Place of Power. A Fae companion can help you navigate the Otherworld and they can also help you work with Fae allies in the physical realm.

With many of my Faerie teachers, there has been encouragement to take on a Fae lover or spouse. I'm actually not really a fan of that practice. Going into the Fae realms with the specific intention of taking an Otherworldly lover feels predatory to me. That's not to say that the relationships that humans have with Fae spouses aren't wonderful or valid, but seeking that out specifically doesn't feel like good ethics to me.

(The concept of ethics is highly personal. Only you can determine what is right for you and what isn't. If you feel in integrity that you can seek out a Fae lover, do so, but be cautious.)

I do find, however, that there is great value in having allies in the Otherworld, and working to develop deep and intimate relationships is very rewarding. I have Fae allies that I have worked with for decades. These are beings that I know well. These are beings that I know intimately, but when our relationship started, intimacy was not my goal. That developed over time.

Having allies in the Otherworld is like having friends or allies in the human realm. We may make friends that we are close to and that relationship is a strong bond that lasts a lifetime. We may also have friends or allies that we have tight bonds with for a shorter amount of time. Friendships and allyships may come and go, they may deepen or dissolve. As you get to know your ally more, you will be able to determine how deep you want to let this ally into your life. You are *always* allowed to say "no, thank you."

If you are doing the following working with a group, have one personal lead the group through the trance process. If you are doing this working alone, record yourself reading the working and listen back to it.

SUPPLIES

There are no specific supplies needed for this ritual. However, put out enough candles so that you don't need electric lighting.

SET UP

This trance is best done on a full moon. I have found this trance to be most effective when it's as close to the Witching hour (midnight) as possible, but at the very least do this working at night. Make sure that you will be undisturbed for at least thirty minutes. Be in a place where you may sit or lie down alone for the duration of the ritual.

RITUAL

Turn off electric lights and light the candles. Cast a simple protective circle, using your fingers to direct the energy. For this working, follow the trance induction.

TRANCE

Open your inner Witch's eye. Before you is the door to your Place of Power. Knock three times, with the intention of finding your Fae ally, and open the door. Step out into the center of your Place of Power. A bright full moon is in the sky above you. Look to see what may have changed since the last time you were here. What can you see, smell, taste, sense on the air in this place? (Pause)

Now look for a trail or path that you may not have noticed before. Allow your feet to carry you to this path and, step by step, begin the journey on this unexplored trail. Notice what stands out on this path. Notice what plants or animals may show up as you continue to walk down this path. Notice any sights or smells as you travel. Keep moving forward, one foot in front of the other, step by step. (Pause)

The path leads to a thick grove of trees, where you wind between and around the thick trunks, the canopy almost blocking out the bright moonlight above you. The light of the moon creates mottled silver shapes along the flat space of the trail. You continue to follow this path through the forest, step by step, one foot in front of the other. Ahead you see an opening in the trees where the moonlight streams through, almost as bright as day.

As you move closer the clearing in the trees becomes clearer. It is awash in moonlight, glowing and Otherworldly. It is a magickal glen, beautiful and shining with power. You enter this glen and feel the kiss of moonlight on your skin. It is like a blessing from the Otherworld. Breathe in this blessing and feel the moonlight sink deeper into your body. (Pause)

Find a place to sit in the clearing and wait. Send out a call from your heart to your Fae ally. From your heart, open up to the being that is ready and willing to work with you now. Feel this calling move out into the Otherworld and wait. (Pause)

There is a rustle in the trees and from the edges of the forest. You see the figure of a Fae being move forward. This being may walk or crawl, they may float or fly. This ally may move quickly or slowly. Just allow their form and shape to come into focus and clarity without trying to force it or push it. As your ally comes closer their shape, form, and physical details become clearer and clearer. (Pause)

Take some time to speak with this ally. Ask them their name. See what wisdom they might have for you at this time. (Pause)

Ask for a token from your Fae ally. Ask for a symbol that they might show you so you can be sure that it is them you are meeting with in the future. This symbol might also show up in the human realm when they want to get ahold of you or have a message for you. (Pause)

Take a moment to ask any other questions that you have. Listen to any other bits of wisdom your Fae ally may have to share with you right now. (Pause)

Time in this place is limited, but know that you can come back here and connect with your Fae ally at any time. For now, take a moment to offer your gratitude, say thank you, and agree to connect with them again soon. (Pause)

When you feel ready, move back to the path that again takes you into the deep forest covering. Follow that path step by step as it moves and winds back through the trees. With one foot in front of the other, follow the trail as it shifts out of the deep cover of the trees. Follow the path as it leads back to the center of your Place of Power.

As you reach the center of your Place of Power, come to the door that leads back to the human realm. Walk through the door and close it behind you. Close your Witch's eye, your inner eye, and step fully back into your body. Breathe deeply and feel the air circulate throughout your body, helping your blood to move through your veins.

Breathe and tap the edges of your body. Breathe and place your hands on the top of your head. Breathe and slowly open your eyes. Breathe and say your name out loud three times.

Welcome back.

FURTHER WORKINGS WITH YOUR ALLY

Here are some ongoing workings that you can try as your relationship with your Fae ally continues:

+ Find out where your Fae ally would prefer to meet with you. They may take you to another place in your Place of Power or a place in their own realm.

+ Ask for their assistance when you are stuck or need guidance on a situation.

+ When you feel like you have gotten to know them better, ask for them to take you to their realm.

+ Ask them to show you signs of their influence in the human realm.

+ Ask to spend time together exploring other areas in your Place of Power.

+ Make space for them in your home or yard.

LEAVE OFFERINGS

Over and over again I hear comments about leaving offerings for the Fae. Some of the talk about offerings can come across sounding like a type of bribery for good behavior given to beings that are prone to shenanigans. Offerings are not about making a payment. And it is a disservice to the Fae to lump them all together, making it sound like they are all potential troublemakers. This is a

Victorian view of fairies that has stuck around in modern popular culture, but it's not an accurate representation of Fae beings, which are much more complex and complicated than a Pixie with attitude stealing your toothbrush.

Offerings are a way to show your willingness to have a relationship. Remember, we are talking about beings that are not of this world in the same way that humans are. Don't expect that your relationships will resemble anything like human relationships. In fact, when it comes to working with the Fae, don't have any expectations at all.

When you leave offerings for the Spirits of the Land where you live, you will notice reciprocity for these gifts. It won't be a gift for a gift, it might not have any rhyme or reason, and you may have to give a lot more than you get—at first—but they will gift you back. They will show their appreciation. They will.

We are so disconnected from them that they might not even realize that you are leaving these offerings for them at first. They are used to being ignored and taken for granted. It might not be initially clear what the best offerings will be. Again, this is something that will depend on the type of Fae you are working with. Figuring all of that out will take time.

Unlike working with deities, in which it is considered okay to eat the offerings after they have been given, it is considered bad form to eat any offerings that you've given to the Fae. When it comes to an offering, once you give it, you never take it back. They have very clear rules about gifting, hosting, and eating.

In the beginning there are a few tried and true offerings. Many of these come from old Irish folktales, and more than a few are holdovers from the Victorian era, when fairies were all the rage; although many of them still work. Some of these offerings have contradictory reactions. I've had Fae teachers (both human and Fae) tell me contrary things. But for the most part, these are items that are more likely to work than not.

+ **Beer:** Not all Fae beings like beer, but my experience is that beer works pretty darn good most of the time. They don't need a tankard full of beer, but a nice cup shows your appreciation.

+ **Whiskey:** This is likely a holdover from Irish folk belief of what to give the Fae, but for the most part, whiskey is a good offering and most often accepted.

+ **Dairy:** Most forms of dairy are pretty good offerings for the Fae. I've yet to meet a Fae being that didn't like dairy, although some prefer meat.

+ **Honey or sweets:** Milk and honey mixed up into a drink is a favorite offering for the Fae, but sweets in general are good options.

+ **Crystals:** This is more of a New Age offering, but crystals work really well. Especially if they are large enough to create a sacred space for the Fae to hang out in.

+ **Plants:** Of course the Fae love plants. They love it even more when they know that a plant is just for them. Just be really sure you can keep the plant alive.

+ **Clean water:** Water may seem simple, but that's why it is such a great offering. Water is my favorite offering because it can also be left out for birds and critters that may need a drink too.

As you start to open up a relationship with the Spirits of the Land, you may find it appropriate to ask questions and deepen the relationship that is forming. When connecting to the Spirits around you, find out how they want your relationship to develop. Ask how they feel about your relationship and what they want. Fae beings may also be able to give you information about the place you live.

QUESTIONS TO ASK THE SPIRITS OF THE LAND:

+ Is my magick welcome here in this place?

+ What sort of magick would be best done in this place to support the Land?

✦ What offerings would be most welcomed?

✦ What magick has been done here before?

✦ How can I best foster a relationship with the Land?

PAY ATTENTION

In every section of relationship building with the Fae, I've talked about paying attention. Not just paying attention to what is in front of you, but also what is happening around you and out of the corner of your eyes.

Not all Fae activity happens in this realm. The Fae have their own realms where they can spend time, undisturbed and unbothered with human activities. But there are places where these boundaries are thin. Some boundaries between our realm and the Fae realm are more like a skin than a wall of bricks and these are the places where their activities may be seen, felt, and experienced, but only if you are paying close enough attention.

THE FAE REALM

As I've said already, until you have a solid relationship with the Fae it is best not to attempt to go wandering around in the Fae realms. They are tricky and difficult to navigate; nothing is what it seems in the Fae realms. However, once you have a Fae companion that can help you, it is much safer.

When you start working with the Spirits of the Land you may find yourself walking into the Fae realms unexpectedly. You may find that a path you've traveled hundreds of times suddenly looks unfamiliar. You could be traveling a path away from a camping spot or gathering and find that you keep walking in circles, unable to get back to where you started. Getting lost in the Fae realms most often looks like getting lost in a place where you should easily not be lost. It is rare and should not be sought out.

There are some tricks for getting out of the Fae realms if you find yourself lost in them. Your best bet is to not wander into these areas at all. However, here are some other tried and true options.

- ✦ Turn your clothes inside out

- ✦ Walk backward

- ✦ Attempt to cross water

"IN" WITH THE FAE

There are some folks who seem to live with one foot in the Otherworld. There are folks with Otherworldly gifts, like the sight, healing, divination, and other spiritual gifts. In folklore and folktales these abilities were connected to the Fae. Those who could see the future or offer healing were said to be "in with the Fae."

Many of us Witches and Pagans work to hone these abilities and gifts. We practice reading tarot cards or opening up to the messages from the Otherworld, but for many cultures across the globe, being Faerie touched was not something you desired. Being touched by the Otherworld could make you a social pariah or, for some ancestors, it could even be dangerous.

Being Faerie touched is not something to be feared, but it is something to take seriously. Experiences with the Fae can change you. It is important that you are spiritually sound, grounded, and practiced before jumping into this kind of work. Having a solid grounding practice and understanding your limits will help to keep you safe. Remember, one of the most powerful spiritual precepts is to know thyself. Understand your limits. Work to strengthen your growing edges.

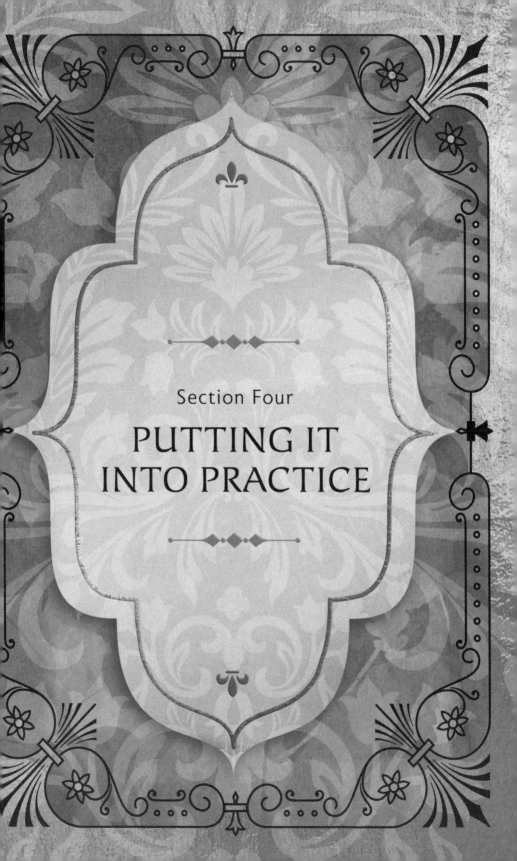

Section Four

PUTTING IT INTO PRACTICE

12

THE WHEEL OF
THE YEAR

It's great to learn about new Godds. It's excellent to develop new skills or get new tips or tricks for your personal practice. However, in my experience, the hardest part of reading a book like this is turning those tips, tricks, or new relationships into daily actionable things to grow personal practice.

A book can be read just for the sake of reading a lovely book without anything else needing to be done or studied. But I find that reading can only bring so much into our practices. Being a Witch is an experiential experience. The best and most powerful learning experiences come not from reading about rituals but from actually doing them.

Here are some ways that you can take the concepts in this book and blend them into your current personal practice or start a brand new personal practice. The goal here is to practice! Try things out, test out these rituals and activities. Modify the offerings here for your own personal pantheon. Shift these rituals or rewrite them to make them fit better into your Pagan practices.

The Godds, the dead, and the Fae are available to work with, worship, or communicate with at any time of the year. There isn't a time of the year that is bad for communion, but there are some times of the year when it is easier to get through to the Otherworlds.

I think about the realms almost like planets in orbit. Each of these realms has its own cycles, times, and seasons. At certain times of the year different realms are closer to each other. Just like certain times of the year, certain planets are closer to each other in orbit. When the realms are closer they can connect and communicate more easily. During specific times of the year the realms of the Otherworlds are easier to communicate with. Messages can be sent and received at any time, but the signal is clearer when you reach out during a closer orbit time.

When you have a solid relationship with a spirit from another realm, this can help make communication easier. Letting the Wheel of the Year influence when you make contact with the Other realms can help you be more successful in your contact. Allow the closer orbits of the different realms to work in your favor, especially when working with a new entity.

The springtime, in the northern hemisphere, is the perfect time of the year to connect with the Fae realms. From Imbolc on February 1, through the Summer Solstice on June 21, the veil to the Fae realms is the easiest to access. The height of this opening is on Beltane, on May 1. This is an excellent time to make new connections to the Fae realms or to open up to the Spirits of the Land where you live.

From Summer Solstice on June 21 through Lammas on August 1 is a time of equilibrium. The realms are accessible, but there is a distance between them. Communication can happen at these times, but it isn't the easiest time for contact to be made.

The fall is the best time of the year to connect with the ancestors. From Lammas on August 1 through the Winter Solstice on December 21, the veil to the ancestral realms is the most accessible. The height of this opening happens on Samhain, on October 31. During what is sometimes called the dark half of the year, you can more easily connect to those that have crossed over, recently or in the distant past.

The time between the Winter Solstice and Imbolc is a fallow time. Although it is always okay to communicate with those entities that you already have a relationship with, it is best not to attempt a new relationship during this time.

The following is a list of days throughout the year when you may want to honor or celebrate the Otherworld. Some of these dates come to us from antiquity, some of them are more modern dates, and I encourage you to create some celebration dates of your own. If there is a day you connect to a specific deity or a creature from the Otherworld, incorporate that date into your personal Wheel of the Year celebrations.

This list of a mixture of celebrations from different cultures and regions across the globe. The goal is to show you how vast and varied celebrations can be. The dates below are a snapshot of different ways to celebrate.

JANUARY

January Full Moon: Thorblot
Make a feast with meat, mead, and fresh bread. Invite friends, relatives, and loved ones over to eat, boast, and toast. It is traditional to toast to your own accomplishments and thank the God Thor for his ever watching eye and guidance.

January 2: Birth of Inanna
Take time to celebrate your senses and sensuality. Do something to pamper yourself. Talk a long bath, get a massage, have a delicious meal, light candles, and listen to calming music. Treat yourself like the Queen of Heaven and Earth. Thank Inanna by offering her cakes.

January 10: Day of Freya
Gather all of your magickal tools, then cleanse and consecrate them to be tools of power. Invoke Freya to guide your magickal work, that all you do may be just and powerful. Use these tools when doing magick for social justice.

FEBRUARY

February Full Moon: Kuan Yin Celebration

On the night of the full moon, set out an altar with an empty bowl and glass of water. Create sacred space in your favorite way, invoking Kuan Yin in the process. Pour into the bowl your heartbreak, your sadness, your stuck places. Pour them out for the Goddess of Compassion. When complete, hold up the glass of water and ask Kuan Yin for her blessings. Let that cup fill up with her compassion. When ready, drink the water and allow it to fill the empty places within you and soothe your soul.

February 1: Imbolc/Brigid's Day

Celebrate Imbolc by having a ritual for Brigid, the Goddess of Inspiration. This is the perfect time of the year to look at what seeds you might want to plant in the coming spring. Sit with Brigid and look at your goals and what you want to manifest. Let Brigid's fire of inspiration fill you.

February 7: Day of Selene

Spend the day honoring the moon. Lay out crystals, plants, and jewelry to ask Selene's blessings. Collect water in honor of the Goddess of the Moon. Read her myths and stories out loud while looking at the moon in the sky. Bonus points if it is close to a full moon.

MARCH

March 4: Chewing Onions for Bast

This is a traditional holiday for the Egyptian Goddess Bastet. Create an altar to this Goddess and spend the day making food, with lots of onions of course! If possible, use onions to decorate the altar. Give Bast offerings of the food. Take time to look at your inner garden. What needs to be pruned or pulled in order to make room for what is growing?

March 17: Festival of Astarte
Build an altar for Astarte using the Star card from your favorite tarot deck. Create sacred space in your favorite way. Trance journey into the Star card and talk to the Goddess in this card. Contemplate the energy of the Star and the energy of the Goddess Astarte. Give her offerings of cakes.

March 30 or the Spring Equinox: Feast of Eostre
Make hard boiled eggs and color or dye them in your favorite way. Draw runes on all of the eggs and then hide them, without paying attention to which runes are hidden where. Invite your friends and family to participate in an egg hunt and read the runes you find as divination for the spring. Only eat the eggs with runes that you want to take on. Give any others as offerings to the Fae and Spirits of the Land.

APRIL

April Full Moon: Gifting the Spirits of the Land
As the energy of spring begins to heat up, it is a good time to give offerings to the Spirits of the Land for their help and guidance. Spend time making treats for the Spirits of the Land and then go out to your favorite spaces and leave them. If weather allows, have a picnic in one of your favorite places and commune with the Spirits there.

April 10: Adoration of Anubis
Put together an altar with beer, bread, and frankincense. Create sacred space in your favorite way, calling on Anubis. He is the great Egyptian psychopomp. Go to your Place of Power and connect with Anubis; ask what you need to transmute. Give him the offerings of bread, beer, and incense.

April 19: Return of Persephone
When Persephone returns to the land, her mother, Demeter, allows life to flourish again. Spend the day honoring Persephone's return by celebrating

what is flourishing in your life. Have fun, play, sing, honor the warmth of spring and the growing things around you.

MAY

April 30 into May 1: Walpurgis Night/Beltane

This is the Witch's Night, while also being the celebration of Saint Walpurgis. Throughout the day, gather nine sacred woods—which may not be an easy feat—and flowers. In the evening, light the sacred fire and make flower wreaths to wear. Celebrate all night with singing, dancing, and feasting around the fire. First thing in the morning, gather the dew outside to be used in ritual and blessing.

May 9: Feast of Artemis

Create an altar for Artemis. Throughout the day cook foods for her. Pour libations of wine, remembering to drink some yourself. As you make preparations, sing to Artemis, ask for her divine blessing. Invite over friends and loved ones to feast in her honor. During the meal, have each person name a trait or goal that they want Artemis to bless with her fierceness. With each naming, pour wine into her offering bowl. When complete, take this out and say a prayer to Artemis, asking a boon of her blessing. Pour out the libation.

May 17: Birth of Apollo

Set up an altar to Apollo with lots of musical instruments. Create sacred space in your favorite way. Call upon Apollo to bless your instruments and then play music for him. It doesn't matter if you know how to play or not, just make noise and have fun.

JUNE

June 15: Make Offerings to Hapi

The Nile inundation is happening and fertility is spreading across the land! Go to a place of running water and set out offerings for Hapi. Pray for fertility and abundance in your own life. Thank Hapi for their life-giving waters.

June 21: Fae Offerings For the Summer Solstice

The veil to the Otherworld is thin. Use this time to connect with your Fae allies or start reaching out to new ones. Spend the day outdoors, watching the activities of the green and red bloods on your land. Leave offerings for the Fae and celebrate their gifts to us.

June 24: Lights of Isis

As Isis searched for Osiris's body, she had to use the glow of magick to help her see at night. Create an altar for Isis with lots of candles. Set sacred space in your favorite way. Call upon Isis to help you see the places where there is darkness in your life. Ask for her assistance to show you the way. Offer a prayer to her as you light each candle on your altar.

JULY

July 10: Day of Hel

Being a Goddess of the Underworld is a hard and often thankless job. Hel, or Hella, of Norse mythology, is often feared because of the power she holds, her realm being the realm of the dead. Create an altar for Hel with bones, dried flowers, and offerings of food and mead. Set sacred space in your favorite way and then call on Hel. Give her offerings and speak your thanks for her realm and her guardianship of the Beloved Dead.

July 15: Chinese Festival of the Dead

This festival is a different day every year, as it is based off of the Chinese calendar rather than the Gregorian calendar. In Chinese mythos this is the day when the gates to the deads' realm is thin and the dead can feast as ghosts. Spend this day at a local cemetery, the older the better. Clean up graves that have fallen into disrepair or have been neglected. Set flowers for the dead. Take your time and give your gratitude for those that have gone before.

July 18: Birthday of Nephthys

The twin sister of Isis, Nephthys was worshipped as the polarity of Isis. On her birthday, set an altar to Nephthys and make her a honey cake. Create sacred space in your favorite way and call upon Nephthys. Ask for her blessing on your shadows, for the pieces of yourself that often go unseen, both positive and negative. Thank her for her power and grace. Give her an offering of the honey cake and beer.

AUGUST

August Full Moon: Festival of Hathor

Also referred to as the festival of drunkenness. This day was a celebration of the roaring wild Goddess Sekhmet becoming drunk on pomegranate beer, thinking it was blood, and waking from her drunken slumber as the gracious (and calm) Hathor. Create an altar to Hathor, including beer. Set sacred space in your favorite way, calling on Hathor. Honor her transformation from rage to benevolence. Call on Hathor to help humankind make that same transition. Give her offerings of beer.

August 1: Lughnasadh, Celebration of Lugh

The Irish God Lugh was known for his skill in almost everything he attempted to do. In myth and lore he often had to put those skills to the test. Spend this day outdoors playing games of competition with loved ones. Have a feast and toast to the winners. Attempt to keep the competition fun and joyful.

August 13: Birthday of Aradia

In some stories, Aradia was a real woman born on August 13 in the year 1313. To honor this moment of magickal confluence, bake a cake for Aradia. Sing "Happy Birthday" to her, offering her the first slice of cake. Say a prayer to all the Witches that have been born since and all the Witches that will continue to be born.

SEPTEMBER

September Full Moon/Autumn Equinox: Celebration of Demeter

As the Greek Goddess of the Land, Demeter can help us to reconnect to the energy of the Land around us. Set an altar for Demeter, including items from the land around you. Create sacred space, calling on Demeter. Journey to your Place of Power to meet Demeter and ask how you can best serve the Land.

September 8: Celebration of Water Spirits

Take water from your tap and go to a local water source: a lake, river, or ocean. Spend time at this place and commune with the Water Spirits that live there. Express your gratitude and pour the water from your home into the water of that place.

September 19: Celebration of Thoth

This is a day of fasting to honor the God of language and wisdom: the Egyptian God Thoth. Consuming only water from sun up until sun down, sit in meditation asking for Thoth to show you the wisdom that you most need right now. When you break your fast, give the first pieces of food as an offering to Thoth.

OCTOBER

October 18: Horned God, Fair

Have a party. The Horned God Fair has a long history in Charlton England. It is believed to have ancient origins connected to the Horned God of Celtic times. Make food, have drinks, encourage partygoers to wear costumes. Celebrate the wild.

October 24: Lilith Day

Wait until dark and then take a spiritual cleansing bath. Use only candlelight, invoke Lilith to guide you and help your cleansing process. Air dry and stay sky-clad while you set up an altar for Lilith. Sit in contemplation on your personal shields and spiritual warding. Travel to your Place of Power to meet Lilith and ask her what you need to do for protection. After getting her advice, return and take steps to complete her suggestions. Give her an offering of red wine.

October 31: Samhain

Have a mummers dinner. Invite friends and family over for an ancestor feast. Everyone should bring a dish of their ancestors. Create sacred space around your dining table, with everyone stepping into silence. Eat your ancestor meal in silence and make sure to give plates to the ancestors.

NOVEMBER

November Full Moon: Baba Yaga Feast Day

One of the impossible tasks Baba Yaga asks of Vasalisa is to cook her food. Have a dinner party and spend the day cooking a large feast or have a potluck and encourage participants to bring foods of their ancestors. In the center of the table place a pot or cauldron filled with charms, stones, trinkets, fortunes, and blessings. As the meal goes on, encourage participants to sort through the pot, picking out charms and fortunes. Give offerings of vodka and food to Baba Yaga.

November 11: Lunatishees

For modern Witches this has become a day to honor the Fae; however, it is important to know that the name of this celebration day comes from a specific kind of Fae that aren't very fond of humans. They guard thorn trees, specifically blackthorn. To honor these beings, take offerings to a blackthorn tree in your area. If there are no blackthorns, take offerings to another type of thorn tree that does grow around you.

November 16: Hecate Night

This is the perfect night to perform a traditional Deipnon, or meal to Hecate. Bonus points if this date falls on a new moon. Take a picnic dinner, after sunset, to a crossroads. Set out the meal as an offering, but do not eat the food;

this is for Hecate only. Pour libations of wine. Take a token as an offering and leave this in the crossroad. Burn cedar as fumigation and cleansing. Call on Hecate and ask for her blessing.

DECEMBER

December 1: Day of Pallas Athena

In one version of the Greek myths, Athena took the epithet *Pallas* after accidentally killing her best friend, Pallas. Set an altar for Athena with an honoring of any grief of your own that you are carrying. Create sacred space in your favorite way, invoking Athena. Express your grief, whether this is through writing, talking, singing, moaning, crying, or keening. Allow the grief to come. Thank Athena for holding your grief and give her offerings of food and wine.

December 21: Feast of Dionysus/Winter Solstice

Dionysus is a Godd that encourages the sensuality of life. Set up your space with an altar for Dionysus and lots of sensual pleasures, including feathers, finger foods and wine, musical instruments, and oils. Encourage participants to dress up in ritual finery. Create sacred space in your favorite way, calling on Dionysus. Revel in the feast of the sensuous. Eat, feed each other, drink, play music, anoint each other with oils, be playful and celebrate life.

December 25: Mithras's Birthday

Yes, Mithras has the same birthday as Jesus. If you celebrate Christmas, add a little Mithrasian worship into the mix. Consider eating your meal while in repose. Have a bull sacrifice. Perhaps go into a cave and contemplate the lost legend while singing praises to the great warrior Mithras. Just kidding, but not about the birthday part—that's true.

DAILY PRACTICE

The concept of daily practice has become something of a buzz word in Witch and Pagan communities. As Witches and Pagans, we don't necessarily have a regimented spiritual practice like you might find in other more dogmatic religions. Paganism and Witchcraft leave a lot of space to create your own personal praxis.

This is part of the magick of walking this path. Being able to mold and create a spiritual routine that is just for you allows space for a practice that actually enlivens and invigorates you. The challenge of this same freedom is the overwhelm of potential or the uncertainty of where to begin, which can lead to not doing a damn thing.

The following daily practice suggestions are just that: suggestions. I encourage you to adjust them, shift them, shake them up, and make them yours.

- **Pick one Godd:** Spend every day just listening for their voice. Find a moment when you can sit undisturbed for at least ten minutes. Call upon them, using your own words. Ask for their guidance and connection. Then just sit and see what comes through. End this with journal writing. Even if all you write is "nothing happened." That's okay, try again tomorrow and keep going.

- **Set offerings:** I've mentioned this a few times, but it is worth mentioning again. If you are going to be in relationship with a deity or Fae being, be prepared to give them offerings. Do this on a daily basis, with as much regular routine as possible.

- **Visit cemeteries:** It is helpful for ancestor work if you can visit the resting places of your own ancestors or Beloved Dead. But if you don't have access to your dead, don't let that stop you from going to cemeteries. Spending time with the dead can help you connect with your own ancestors. Spending time at a cemetery can also help you become more comfortable working with those that have crossed over. Plus, older cemeteries are really beautiful. Many rural or old cemeteries will offer guided tours or history nights when you can learn about some of the people buried there.

- **Do rituals:** Do daily rituals, weekly rituals, monthly rituals, annual rituals. Do these rituals and include your deities, dead, and the Spirits of your Land. Take time to write invocations or poetry for those of the Otherworlds that you want to connect with. Allow these to be as elaborate or simple as you feel called to offer.

+ **Spend time outdoors:** If you're looking to explore relationship with the Spirits of the Land, the ancestors, or the Godds, you will find that being outdoors gives you a connection to the world around you. Breathe fresh air, listen to birds, feel the wind, get wet from rain, let the sun kiss your skin. Remember that you are made of the earth; let yourself connect to feeling what that means, even if you can only do that sitting in the open window of your apartment in a major city.

+ **Learn language:** Go back to the country of origin of the deity you want to work with or where your ancestors may be from, and learn that language. Of course, some languages are dead, so what might be the modern equivalent of that language? Start there. There are plenty of apps and programs that make learning a new language easy (or easier). Then you can practice what you've learned in ritual.

+ **Speak to them:** With the Godds, the ancestors, and the Fae it is important to keep communication going all the time. Spend time talking to those you are in relationship with on a daily basis. You can't text them, like you would a human friend with a phone, but you can keep the lines of communication open.

Our world is full of magick, and we all have access to it. The entities in the Otherworlds are just as curious about us as we are about them. It is our duty to tell the stories, sing the songs, and dance the dances. It is our responsibility as Witches and Pagans to say "what is remembered lives" when someone crosses over. It is up to us to help keep these energies strong and alive in this world.

Even when involved with a coven or community, walking this path can sometimes be lonely or isolating. We can have a group experience, but more often than not we have a personal experience. Those that dwell in the Otherworlds understand these things. You don't have to try to explain what you mean. You don't have to try to be someone you're not. Working with entities from other realms allows us to be who we are while digging in deep and doing the work on connectivity.

Let this magick help you grow and expand. Let it connect you to the mystery and power of the world around you.

BIBLIOGRAPHY

Armand, Khi. *Deliverance.* Forestville: Lucky Mojo, 2015.

Adler, Margot. *Drawing Down the Moon.* New York: Penguin Books, 1986.

Bulfinch, Thomas. *Bulfinch's Mythology.* New York: Crown Publishers, 1979.

Conway, DJ. *Moon Magick.* St. Paul: Llewellyn, 1995.

Cooper, Jason D. *Mithras Mysteries and Initiation Rediscovered.* York Beach: Samuel Weiser, 1996.

Crowley, Vivianne. *Way of Wicca.* London: HarperCollins, 2001.

Cunningham, Scott. *Encyclopedia of Magical Herbs.* St. Paul: Llewellyn, 1994.

Daimler, Morgan. *Pagan Portals Brigid.* Hants: Moon Books, 2016.

Dominguez Jr., Ivo. *Spirit Speak.* Franklin Lakes: New Page , 2008.

Foor, Daniel Ph.D. *Ancestors Medicine.* Rochester: Bear & Co, 2017.

Fortune, Dion. *Applied Magic.* York Beach: Samuel Weiser, 2000.

———. *Moon Magic.* San Francisco: Red Wheel/Weiser, 2003.

Gardner, Gerald. *The Meaning of Witchcraft.* Boston: Red Wheel/Weiser, 2004.

———. *Witchcraft Today.* New York: Citadel Press, 2004.

Griffiths, Bill. *Aspects of Anglo-Saxon Magic.* Norfolk: Anglo-Saxon Books, 2006.

Heselton, Philip. *Witchfather*. Leicestershire, UK: Thoth Publications, 2012.

Hillman, James. *The Soul's Code*. New York: Random House, 1996.

Kadmon, Baal. *The Magick of Lilith*. Baal Kadmon, 2016.

Koltuv Ph. D., Barbara Black. *The Book of Lilith*. Newburyport: Weiser, 1986.

Kubler-Ross, Elizabeth and David Kessler. *On Grief and Grieving*. New York: Scribner, 2005.

Larrington, Carolyne. *The Poetic Edda*. New York: Oxford Press, 1996.

LeFae, Phoenix. *Hoodoo Shrines and Altars*. Forestville: MISC, 2015.

Leland, Charles G. *Aradia or The Gospel of the Witches*. Unknown: Global Grey, 1899.

Lenihan, Eddie and Carolyn Eve Green. *Meeting the Other Crowd*. New York: Penguin, 2004.

Matthews, Caitlin and Jon. *Ladies of the Lake*. London: The Aquarian Press, 1992.

Monaghan, Patricia. *Brigit: Sun of Womanhood*. Las Vegas: Goddess Ink, 2013.

Moura, Ann. *Grimoire for the Green Witch*. St. Paul: Llewellyn, 2003.

Murray, Margaret A. *The Splendour That Was Egypt*. London: Biddles, 1984.

Naydler, Jeremy. *Temple of the Cosmos*. Rochester: Inner Traditions, 1996.

Paxon, Diana L. *Taking Up the Runes*. San Francisco: Weiser, 2005.

Phillips, Julia. "G.B. Gardner." Accessed 9/10/2018. Geraldgardner.com.

Richardson, Alan. *The Magical Life of Dion Fortune*. London: Aquarian Press, 1991.

Starhawk and Nightmare, M. Macha. *Pagan Book of Living and Dying*. San Francisco: HarperCollins, 1997.

Wolkstein, Diane. *Inanna Queen of Heaven and Earth*. New York: Harper & Row, 1983.

CONTRIBUTOR BIOS

Gede Parma (Fio Aengus) is a Balinese-Australian Witch, author, priestess, professional Witchcraft teacher, cunning person, and diviner. They are the author of *Ecstatic Witchcraft*, *By Land, Sky & Sea*, and *Spirited*, as well as co-author of *Magic of the Iron Pentacle* with Jane Meredith, and co-editor of *Elements of Magic*. They are initiated and work within the Wildwood, Reclaiming, and Anderson Feri Traditions of Witchcraft.

Suzanne Sterling is a musician, yogi, and activist who has been performing and teaching transformational workshops for over twenty-five years. She is founder of Voice of Change, inspiring others to find their unique voice as a tool for conscious evolution. Suzanne has been featured at hundreds of international festivals and conference centers including Omega, Esalen, Wanderlust, Kripalu, Symbiosis, Bhaktifest, and many more. Since 2007 she has been training leaders in spiritual activism and social justice through her co-founded organization, Off The Mat, Into the World. As director of the Seva Challenge, which raised over $4 million, she has spent time in the US, India, Cambodia, Haiti, Ecuador, and Africa working in community resilience. For twenty-five years, she has worked with the International Reclaiming Community, creating ritual, training teachers, and offering yearlong Sacred Leadership trainings. She has released five solo albums and numerous DVD soundtracks (www.suzannesterling.com).

Alicia Foster-Scales, also known as the Writ Witch, is a passionate writer, poet, and storyteller, creating poetry as a spiritual offering and as a means of better coming to know deity. As a student of the Reclaiming Tradition of Witchcraft and a practitioner of rootwork, Alicia's omnist and pantheist perspective on spirituality and life itself is grounded in the importance of Story and Myth in understanding not only who we are and who we've been, but also who we have the potential to be. As the Writ Witch, she writes custom devotional and narrative poetry and offers dream interpretations, as well as delving into bibliomancy and rhapsodomancy as daily practice. An avid researcher, belly dance performer, doula, and activist for comprehensive sex education and reproductive rights, Alicia works primarily with Lilith, Persephone, and her ancestors.

TO WRITE TO THE AUTHOR

If you wish to contact the author or would like more information about this book, please write to the author in care of Llewellyn Worldwide Ltd. and we will forward your request. Both the author and publisher appreciate hearing from you and learning of your enjoyment of this book and how it has helped you. Llewellyn Worldwide Ltd. cannot guarantee that every letter written to the author can be answered, but all will be forwarded. Please write to:

Phoenix LeFae
℅ Llewellyn Worldwide
2143 Wooddale Drive
Woodbury, MN 55125-2989

Please enclose a self-addressed stamped envelope for reply,
or $1.00 to cover costs. If outside the U.S.A., enclose
an international postal reply coupon.

Many of Llewellyn's authors have websites with additional information and resources. For more information, please visit our website at http://www.llewellyn.com.

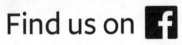

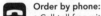